THE WORLD'S FINEST CIGARS

PHOTOGRAPHS BY MATTHIEU PRIER

Flammarion

Antoni Vives Fierro. *Tobacco Sorters*. Oil on canvas.

CONTENTS

Non-Cuban cigars are followed by the initials of their country of origin (C: Canary Islands; D: Dominican Republic; H: Honduras; N: Nicaragua).

Pirámide, Campana, Exquisito
6   Cohiba Millennium 2000
7   Diplomáticos N°2
8   H. Upmann N°2
9   Montecristo N°2
10 Partagás Pirámides Limited Edition
11 San Cristóbal de La Habana La Punta
12 Vegas Robaina Únicos
13 Bolívar Belicosos Finos
14 Romeo y Julieta Belicosos
15 Arturo Fuente Hemingway Reserva Especial Signature (D)
16 Santa Damiana Torpedo (D)
17 Cuaba Exclusivos

Gran Corona
18 Hoyo de Monterrey Particulares Limited Edition
19 Montecristo "A"

Prominente
20 Hoyo de Monterrey Double Coronas
21 Partagás Lusitanias
22 Punch Double Coronas
23 Ramón Allones Gigantes
24 Romeo y Julieta Exhibición N°2 Limited Edition
25 Vegas Robaina Don Alejandro

Julieta
26 Bolívar Coronas Gigantes Cabinet Selection
27 La Gloria Cubana Taínos

28 H. Upmann Sir Winston
29 Punch Churchills
30 Quai d'Orsay Imperiales
31 El Rey del Mundo Taínos
32 Romeo y Julieta Churchills
33 Saint Luis Rey Churchills
34 San Cristóbal de La Habana El Morro

Corona Gorda
35 Montecristo Coronas Grandes (D)
36 Cohiba Siglo IV
37 Hoyo de Monterrey Épicure N°1
38 H. Upmann Magnum 46
39 Juan López Selección N°1
40 Punch Royal Selection N°11
41 Punch Black Prince
42 Punch Super Selection N°2
43 Rafael González Coronas Extra
44 Saint Luis Rey Série A
45 San Cristóbal de La Habana La Fuerza

Hermoso N°4, Robusto, others
46 H. Upmann Connoisseur N°1
47 El Rey del Mundo Cabinet Selección Choix Suprême
48 Romeo y Julieta Exhibición N°4 Cabinet Selección
49 Saint Luis Rey Regios
50 Arturo Fuente Fuente Opus X Perfexción Robustos (D)
51 Flor de Copán Rothschild 50 x 5 (H)
52 Vega Fina Robustos (D)

53	Bolívar Royal Coronas		76	Bolívar Petit Coronas Cabinet Selection
54	Cohiba Robustos		77	Cohiba Siglo II
55	Juan López Selección N°2		78	Hoyo de Monterrey Le Hoyo du Prince
56	Montecristo Robustos Limited Edition		79	Partagás Petit Coronas Cabinet Selection
57	Partagás Série D N°4		80	Por Larrañaga Petit Coronas Cabinet Selection
58	Ramón Allones Specially Selected		81	Punch Petit Coronas
59	S.T. Dupont Robustos (C)		82	Punch Royal Selection N°12
			83	Rafael González Petit Coronas
			84	Ramón Allones Petit Coronas
			85	Saint Luis Rey Petit Coronas

Dalia

60	Bolívar Inmensas
61	Cohiba Siglo V
62	La Gloria Cubana Médaille d'Or N°2
63	Ramón Allones 8-9-8 Varnished

Minuto

86	Partagás Shorts
87	Ramón Allones Small Club Coronas
88	San Cristóbal de La Habana El Príncipe

Cervantes

64	Partagás Lonsdales Cabinet Selection
65	Rafael González Lonsdales
66	Sancho Panza Molinos

Laguito

89	Cohiba Lanceros
90	Trinidad Fundadores

Corona Grande

67	Cohiba Siglo III
68	La Gloria Cubana Sabrosos
69	Hoyo de Monterrey Le Hoyo des Dieux
70	Punch Super Selection N°1

Delicado

91	La Gloria Cubana Médaille d'Or N°1

Panetela Larga

92	La Gloria Cubana Médaille d'Or N°3
93	Rafael González Slenderellas

Corona Mareva and Almuerzo

71	Partagás Coronas Cabinet Selection
72	Ramón Allones Coronas Cabinet Selection
73	Romeo y Julieta Coronas
74	Sancho Panza Coronas
75	Padrón 1964 Anniversary Coronas (N)

94	Index

To my father, who handed down the passion.

PREFACE

The idea of representing all the world's greatest cigars is an impossibly gargantuan challenge. In taking up the gauntlet nevertheless, it is interesting to notice the revolutions, changes and mutations in the universe of cigars, as well as the eternal truths. While every year—every day—brings innovations, the great classics stand tall, their excellence assures their perennial place of honor.

Since a selection must be made, how do we go about choosing? All of the cigars presented in this book come from our aging rooms. This means they have been conserved under ideal conditions that allow them to live up to their full potential. We used a process of elimination, opting only for those cigars with that special something that sets them apart from the others, however excellent in quality. Finally, the heart has its say. In the final analysis, we are aficionados who have our own personal preferences, leanings, nostalgia—just like you.

A few comments on our rating system are in order. The term "power" is meant to indicate strength, but also richness of flavor. "Uniformity" is judged in terms of a cigar's fabrication (suppleness, how tightly packed, porosity) and draw, which is essential to the art of smoking. The "character" rating is intended as a point of comparison, not an absolute. All the cigars discussed in these pages are of the highest quality, a term that also bears some defining. A cigar may be impeccable in terms of its tobacco, manufacturing, finish, and maturation, and still not make our final cut. As with any judgement, relativity plays a role. A young vitola can improve greatly in the aging process, an older cigar may have fallen by the wayside and benefit from a reevaluation of its virtues, and time can bring a new verdict on what was long considered an indisputable first choice. Above all, the finest outcomes result from minute differences, subtleties and nuances which bear noting, to the best of our ability, for the consumer in all of us.

The "Enjoyment" category is designed to provide all the necessary information for optimal smoking pleasure. This includes historical points, affinities with food, wine, alcohol, and circumstances, and suitability with regard to degree of cigar smoking experience. The aim is to sharpen the aficionado's perceptive and analytical skills.

Throughout this book, our one wish is that you finish reading it with your taste buds alerted and your senses awakened, eager to sample one of these, or perhaps some other cigar. This is because we know that a fine cigar demands attention, care, and constant alertness—in other words passion—to reach its peak. But we also know that the best preparation for savoring a cigar is to dream about it. We hope that this book can be the stuff that dreams are made of.

Pirámide - Cuba -

COHIBA MILLENNIUM 2000

Length: 6⅛ in. (156 mm)
Ring Gauge: 52 (20.64 mm)
Body: round
Presentation: jar of 25

Look
The special ring on these well-constructed torpedos bears the distinguishing "2000" inscription. The blend of *colorado* and *maduro* leaves evoke strength.

Touch
Cigars in this family are rough and oily to the touch. The elongated body complements the perfectly conical head.

Smell
The packaging—in a jar—provides an olfactory bonus. The initial, fresh odor yields to stronger, cacao aromas and good, heavy staying-power.

Taste
The Millennium's taste is distinctively rich, powerful, round, and deep. The harsher notes develop prior to aging, and the last third overheats, but attentive aging can dissipate these flaws to release the slightly earthy, spiced aroma of this unusually aromatic Cohiba.

Enjoyment
Issued as a commemorative cigar for the year 2000, this handsome model should be matured for several years before smoking. Once it reaches its peak, it will be great to savor with a fine wine of the same vintage; preferably a Haut-Brion, Lafite, or Petrus.

OVERALL RATING
Strength: 8½ – Uniformity: 9 – Character: 8½

Pirámide - Cuba -

DIPLOMÁTICOS N°2

Length: 6⅛ in. (156 mm)
Ring Gauge: 52 (20.64 mm)
Body: square
Presentation: traditional box of 25

Look
This rich and full vitola is well-built, with a particularly finely finished head. The *colorado claro* and *maduro* versions both exude strength.

Touch
Flexible rather than soft, this cigar's energetic charge is highlighted by the unctuous mix of humidity and natural fleshiness.

Smell
The rich, long-lasting floral aroma is almost harsh in the first two years, but gains in roundness and nobility as it matures.

Taste
From the first puff, the deep, strong taste might even be overwhelming for a cigar novice. This cigar can be set aside for a few minutes at the sublime mid-point, to enhance the finely concentrated finish, where the humid, spicy aromas turn more woodsy. But the powerful, somewhat hot combustion requires expertise.

Enjoyment
The Diplomáticos N°2 was formerly eclipsed by the format's brighter stars, but has come into its own in the past decade. It is divine for after-dinner smoking, especially when accompanied by a fine digestive liqueur. Proper aging will soften the initial punch.

OVERALL RATING
Strength: 8½ – Uniformity: 8 – Character: 7½

Pirámide - Cuba -

H. UPMANN N°2

Length: 6⅛ in. (156 mm)
Ring Gauge: 52 (20.64 mm)
Body: square
Presentation: traditional box of 25

Look
A cigar with a definite presence, the H. Upmann N°2's commonly *colorado* wrappers display charismatic red and brown tones. Some more highly veined leaves stand out amid the box's exceptional regularity.

Touch
This is a rigid, compact, homogeneously constructed cigar. Its even foot gives way to a stout body with a perfect pointed copula of a head. Its velvety texture leaves a slight oily film on the skin. Imposing, firm, and masculine.

Smell
The powerful spicy aroma emerges from an amber base to yield the first joys of savoring. The bouquet is marked by highly humid and developed woodsy underbrush notes.

Taste
From the first draw, the flavor is deeply rich and unctuously strong. The H. Upmann N°2 is exceptionally long in the mouth. The accent is on spicy, peppery, pungent taste, along the traditional lines of the torpedo format.

Enjoyment
It was years before this great figurado took its rightful place beside the venerable Montecristo N°2. Contrary to its appearance, the H. Upmann N°2 is in no way heavy. It is a fine complement to a rich meal for an experienced connoisseur, but not recommended for the novice or occasional smoker.

OVERALL RATING
Strength: 9 – Uniformity: 8½ – Character: 9

Pirámide - Cuba -

MONTECRISTO N°2

Length: 6⅛ in. (156 mm)
Ring Gauge: 52 (20.64 mm)
Body: square
Presentation: traditional box of 25

Look
The color range of this king of torpedos runs the gamut of light to dark, with consistent oiliness. The *colorado* is the best-looking of the bunch.

Touch
A perfect body, at once supple and tensed, with the head worthy of a goldsmith. It feels so good in your hand that you'll think you are holding a double corona.

Smell
Immediate and rich, with a spiciness uncharacteristic of the brand. The body exudes a slight leatheriness, while the foot has its own full measure of woodsy, round, rich flavor.

Taste
The first third is more generous than flavorful. Real tastes kick in from there, with striking woodsy, leather, and humid earthy aromas that build into an unguent, spiced finale heightened by the conical tip.

Enjoyment
Often criticized, the Montecristo N°2 remains a great cigar when properly manufactured. This highly distinctive cigar is in a class of its own, and not to be judged by comparison. Perfect after a fine, rich meal along with a unique wine, one that is evocative of sun-drenched climes.

OVERALL RATING
Strength: 9 – Uniformity: 8½ – Character: 8½

Pirámide - Cuba -

PARTAGÁS PIRÁMIDES LIMITED EDITION

Length: 6⅛ in. (156 mm)
Ring Gauge: 52 (20.64 mm)
Body: square
Presentation: traditional box of 25

Look
The wrapper leaves, full of sunlight and sap, give this grand Havana its oily richness and density. The dark brown hue, laced with reddish earth tones, heralds this cigar's overall rough and robust style.

Touch
Supple yet firm, with a velvety, slightly rough texture and a masterfully regular head.

Smell
The body gives off an aroma of new leather, while the foot intoxicates with its complex, spicy fragrance. Habit-forming.

Taste
Havana in all its glory, with the authentic taste of the 1940s and 1950s. Rich, strong, and tannic from the word go. The characteristic spiciness is a favorite of connoisseurs.

Enjoyment
Manufacturing on this limited edition cigar, with its *edición limitada* ring, ran through 2001. It has the power and style which is a hallmark of fine Havana tradition. Ideal for long winter evenings, the kind for reinventing the world beside a roaring fire, to be sipped with strong spirits. This cigar will age beautifully.

OVERALL RATING
Strength: 10 – Uniformity: 9 – Character: 9½

Pirámide - Cuba -

SAN CRISTÓBAL DE LA HABANA LA PUNTA

Length: 6⅛ in. (156 mm)
Ring Gauge: 52 (20.64 mm)
Body: square
Presentation: traditional box of 25

Look
On par with the great torpedos. The San Cristóbal La Punta's silky wrappers range from noble gold to rich red tonalities.

Touch
The uniform construction highlights the leaves' unctuous richness, with a velvety smoothness in the darker colors.

Smell
This cigar is still too young to have come into its own, aroma-wise. The foot's bouquet is green and floral.

Taste
The smooth, aromatic start develops into a powerful, rich second third, with a strong finale. Great performance for such a young vitola, without the overheating common to fledgling cigars.

Enjoyment
The La Punta is a product of the late 1990s, when this type of format was in fashion. It is an excellent addition to an ambitious line with fine unctuousness, staying power, and medium-deep richness. The La Punta is a good choice for dinner with a tannic, woodsy, slightly smoky red wine.

OVERALL RATING
Strength: 7 – Uniformity: 8 – Character: 7½

Pirámide - Cuba -

VEGAS ROBAINA ÚNICOS

Length: 6⅛ in. (156 mm)
Ring Gauge: 52 (20.64 mm)
Body: square
Presentation: traditional box of 25

Look
This cigar's color is often *claro* or *colorado;* sometimes *maduro.* The handsome gold and brown ring and the veined wrapper leaves make for a distinctive appearance.

Touch
Bulky and packed without over-stuffing, with a delicate smooth surface, good rigidity, and suppleness to boot.

Smell
The foot's subtle green and humid earth nuances yield to rustic, fleshy earth aromas, still with a vegetal note, but never floral.

Taste
This is the new brand's most powerful model. The traditional flavor is apparent from the outset, and may be too much for beginners. The rich, heavy taste becomes strong and spicy in the smoking. Roundness and smoothness will improve after a few years' aging.

Enjoyment
For the lover of raw sensations, this generous cigar goes straight to the point of its full flavor. It is ideal after a hearty game dinner, along with a great Armagnac.

OVERALL RATING
Strength: 9 – Uniformity: 7 – Character: 6½

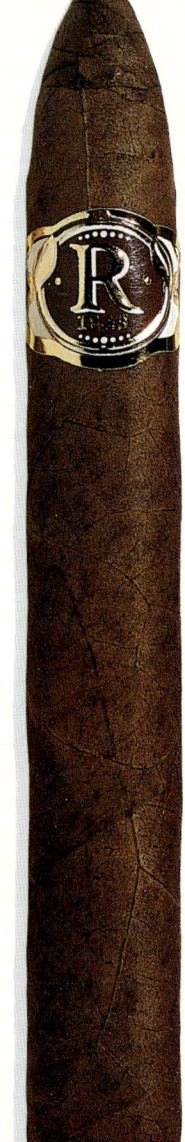

Campana - Cuba -

BOLÍVAR BELICOSOS FINOS

Length: 5½ in. (140 mm)
Ring Gauge: 52 (20.64 mm)
Body: round
Presentation: cabinet of 25; traditional box of 25

Look
The cabinet selection displays rhythmically bound packets of chocolaty rods, in hues running the gamut from soft ocher to deep browns, tinged with gold and even green.

Touch
Thick and tender, with a winning suppleness. The perfect ratio between length and girth makes the Belicosos Finos a joy in the hand.

Smell
A full, rich, bouquet of woodsy spices.

Taste
In true torpedo style, the Belicosos Finos starts out smooth, with rich, if fleeting, flavor which develops with stronger, deliciously round, spiced aromas. The conical head lends staying power to the potent finale.

Enjoyment
This torpedo lacks the instantaneous impact and rapid evolution of the robusto model, but makes up for it in complexity, appearance, and bold finish. Good for after-lunch or daytime smoking for spicy-taste lovers. Alcohol does nothing for this cigar. It's a fine vintage on its own.

OVERALL RATING
Strength: 7½ – Uniformity: 9 – Character: 8

• In the same family, the **Sancho Panza Belicosos** is milder and far more floral.

Campana - Cuba -

ROMEO Y JULIETA BELICOSOS

Length: 5½ in. (140 mm)
Ring Gauge: 52 (20.64 mm)
Body: square
Presentation: traditional box of 25

Look
The outstandingly homogeneous, barely veined wrappers make this campana look fit for a king. Deep tones and perfect texture, very oily but not excessively so.

Touch
Elegantly plump, with an elfin head. When not too tightly packed, this cigar is pleasing in the hand; ideally supple and responsive.

Smell
The foot's ample bouquet is distinct from the body's soft leather aroma. Consummately smooth; never cloying.

Taste
From the start, pedigree woodsy spiced flavor, with voluptuous volumes. This is the kind of cigar that leaves you wanting more. When properly made, it burns perfectly, enhanced by the fine torpedo head.

Enjoyment
If only it were a couple of inches longer! This savory cigar leaves you begging for more. Perfect with fish on a fine summer evening, lakeside, with a fruity white wine.

OVERALL RATING
Strength: 7 – Uniformity: 8 – Character: 9

Figurado - Dominican Republic -

ARTURO FUENTE HEMINGWAY RESERVA ESPECIAL SIGNATURE

Length: 6 in. (152 mm)
Ring Gauge: 48 (19 mm)
Body: round
Presentation: semi-varnished box of 25, individually cellophane wrapped

Look
Ringed in red and gold and girded in gilted black, this handsome, self-assured model sports dark brown, expertly crafted wrappers.

Touch
Supple outside, slightly rigid and crackly inside, with a good feel in the hand. The texture is smooth, more silky than oily, and the highly uniform wrapper leaf is finely grained.

Smell
Markedly floral, round, and abrupt, typical of the brand. The smooth aroma evaporates to a slightly dusty finish.

Taste
Refreshingly straightforward; head-on. Initially a bit dry in the mouth, the flavor develops into rounder, woodsy pleasure, with a discreet richness in the final third.
Excellent combustion adds fullness without overheating.

Enjoyment
A worthy representative of the new generation of smooth, easy cigars, the Hemingway Reserva Especial Signature makes a good morning smoke, or for those with the time, can be savored throughout the day.

OVERALL RATING
Strength: 6½ – Uniformity: 8½ – Character: 7½

Figurado - Dominican Republic -

SANTA DAMIANA TORPEDO

Length: 6¼ in. (159 mm)
Ring Gauge: 48 (19 mm)
Body: round
Presentation: traditional box of 25

Look
Perfectly symmetrical, with a slightly elongated head which makes for a quicker start. The light golden color is set off by a lovely blue-toned ring.

Touch
Consistent and smooth rather than oily. With a nice heft in the hand. Slightly packed yet supple, especially at the perfectly round foot.

Smell
Primarily vegetal at the foot; honeyed and round in the body. The fragrance is volatile and fleeting, with a lingering freshness uncommon in this format.

Taste
Sweet, smooth start, with a hint of dryness that opens into rich, understated elegance. Flavor builds in the last third to heady, exotic strength.

Enjoyment
This torpedo is a good introduction for newcomers to the format, and makes a fine daytime smoke for those in the know. Perfect after a summer dinner; never tiring.

OVERALL RATING
Strength: 7 – Uniformity: 7½ – Character: 7½

• For similar aroma in the same family, try the **Vega Fina Pirámide**.

Exquisito - Cuba -

CUABA EXCLUSIVOS

Length: 5¾ in. (145 mm)
Ring Gauge: 45 (17.82 mm)
Body: round
Presentation: traditional box of 25

Look
At a glance, reminiscent of the old-fashioned nineteenth-century Dutch cigar, but the gold inscribed ring, and above all the tobacco, reveal its contemporary spirit.

Touch
Consistent, though tighter at the head than the foot. Firm, with a fine bearing that is not only the effect of its narrowness.

Smell
Fresh and floral, with a dry note. Down to earth. The body brims with slightly acrid hints of fern and green pepper.

Taste
A unique freshness, midway between dry and light, highlights this cigar's woodsy aroma—the most pronounced in the line. The slow start, due to architectonics, builds to the smooth and consistent combustion which makes this model a boon to newcomers.

Enjoyment
The deft mix of sensual elegance, which is hard to pull off, makes the Cuaba Exclusivos a fine addition to this great collection of Cuban cigars.

OVERALL RATING
Strength: 6 – Uniformity: 7 – Character: 6½

• *In the same family, the* **Partagás Presidentes** *is stronger, longer, and slightly thicker.*

Gran Corona - Cuba -

HOYO DE MONTERREY PARTICULARES LIMITED EDITION

Length: 9¼ in. (235 mm)
Ring Gauge: 47 (18.65 mm)
Body: round
Presentation: traditional box of 5 in wooden holders

Look
The elegance and beauty of rich, thick *maduro* tones enhance its imposing length.

Touch
Rich and silky, consistent and resistant. Solidity only minimally compromises suppleness.

Smell
The initially discreet mildness gives way to potent richness, and finishes on a floral, woodsy note.

Taste
True to cigars of these proportions, the Particulares Limited Edition starts off mild, with grassy muted flavor. A sustained woodsyness dominates the second third, with a hint of non-vegetal spice that deepens in the smoking.

Enjoyment
The prolonged smoking time necessary, largely the result of its compactness, may tire out the novice. However, this cigar is surprisingly manageable for its format. At its best after dinner or with a long winter lunch.

OVERALL RATING
Strength: 8 – Uniformity: 7 – Character: 7

• In the same family, the **Sancho Panza Sanchos** is mellower and lighter in the mouth, with less presence.

Gran Corona - Cuba -

MONTECRISTO "A"

Length: 9¼ in. (235 mm)
Ring Gauge: 47 (18.65 mm)
Body: round
Presentation: semi-varnished box of 25

Look
"A" for art in cigar crafting. Whether blond, brown, or dark brown in color, this stunning *especial* sports fine wrappers, masterfully modeled. A jewel in its varnished wood box.

Touch
Silky and smooth, but never soft. Consistent suppleness from foot to head.

Smell
The savory, persistent bouquet penetrates with mellow, lightly woodsy aromas, in a mix of discreet insistence and imposing presence.

Taste
From a nearly imperceptible beginning for this format, the distinct phases are clearly distinguishable. Early vegetal flavor expands to strong woodsy, honeyed leather, and peppery sensations, with a potently spiced yet elegant finale. The transitions are smooth, with silky, melting flavor.

Enjoyment
This mythic model has occasionally suffered in public opinion due to its format. It remains an after-dinner institution to be lingered over. Inexperienced palates tend to be overwhelmed by the Montecristo "A", especially when accompanied with alcohol. The "A" matures beautifully, gaining in roundness and mellowness, and its woodsy note on a Madera backdrop is typical of great vintages.

OVERALL RATING
Strength: 8 – Uniformity: 9 – Character: 9½

Prominente - Cuba -

HOYO DE MONTERREY DOUBLE CORONAS

Length: 7⅝ in. (194 mm)
Ring Gauge: 49 (19.45 mm)
Body: round
Presentation: cabinet of 50; traditional box of 25

Look
Though also available in a box of 25, the cabinet selection, with its 50 bound beauties, is a sight for sore eyes. The uncommonly elegant and uniform gold wrappers encase a silky, unctuous tobacco.

Touch
This generous cigar, with its velvety texture, is like fine silk in the hand. When well preserved, it breathes so beautifully that light pressure gives the illusion of permeability.

Smell
The cabinet selection offers an incomparable unfolding of mild, round, silky gingerbread aromas. Faint at first, the fragrance builds in a rich, persistent intensity of mild spices.

Taste
The heart of this Havana. After an unassuming beginning, a bloom of floral, slightly woodsy taste, never heavy-handed. Roundness and generosity are this venerable model's two pillars of taste.

Enjoyment
With its rare architectural purity of construction, this pedigree grandee is perfect for fish, accompanied by a great white Burgundy.

OVERALL RATING
Strength: 7 – Uniformity: 9 – Character: 9½

Prominente - Cuba -

PARTAGÁS LUSITANIAS

Length: 7⅝ in. (194 mm)
Ring Gauge: 49 (19.45 mm)
Body: round
Presentation: cabinet of 50; traditional box of 25

Look
A superb bound bunch running the gilded gamut from light gold to burnished brown. Aesthetic perfection from foot to head.

Touch
Luxurious, velvety wrappers envelope the silky, rich tobacco with high drama. A show-stopper body, at once supple and taut.

Smell
A brilliantly nuanced palate of unguent, woodsy potency, marked by generous leather textures. Invigorating in young cigars, rounding with maturity to a broad mellowness, sometimes with a pinch of cinnamon.

Taste
Piercing in the young Lusitanias, with potent woodsy and spiced aromas. The range expands into heavier, more vegetal flavors, without giving up on spiciness. The finale crescendos to a veritable fireworks.

Enjoyment
Unheard of thirty years ago, the Lusitanias is considered a must for this format today. This eclectic cigar goes equally well with a lavish gourmet meal or rustic fare. Best smoked from May to October, with a break in the winter.

OVERALL RATING
Strength: 9½ – Uniformity: 9 – Character: 9½

Prominente - Cuba -

PUNCH DOUBLE CORONAS

Length: 7⅝ in. (194 mm)
Ring Gauge: 49 (19.45 mm)
Body: round
Presentation: cabinet of 50; traditional box of 25

Look
Breathtakingly gorgeous. This superb rod is state of the art in potency, richness, and pedigree elegance, lending it an exceptional vitality.

Touch
Heavy, compact, strong and yet delicate, with a masculine silkiness, at times a bit oily and charged.

Smell
The scent of a lifetime; one that should never end. The range is rich and complex, with unctuous, woodsy odors on an earthy base. A whole forest of intertwined, meandering olfactory paths.

Taste
The gift of full force from the start. The aromatic register is played out in mild, slightly woodsy flavor which crescendos to a veritable apotheosis that leaves a salty hint on the lips.

Enjoyment
A vitola for the great moments in life, alone or accompanied, but in utter devotion to the cult of smoking. Perfect after an exquisite dinner. This cigar may be a bit much for new smokers. It ages excellently.

OVERALL RATING
Strength: 8½ – Uniformity: 8 – Character: 9

• In the same family, the **Saint Luis Rey Prominente** is a marvel of craftsmanship and raw materials, but hard to come by.

Prominente - Cuba -

RAMÓN ALLONES GIGANTES

Length: 7⅝ in. (194 mm)
Ring Gauge: 49 (19.45 mm)
Body: round
Presentation: traditional box of 25

Look
Usually in *maduro* tones, deep and imposing. The red and gold ring highlights the pleasingly rounded head.

Touch
Supremely silky, rigid and tensed, with a supple bounce that saves it from excessive hardness.

Smell
Smoked before maturity, the Gigantes wafts hints of new leather and dew-drenched flowers. The eager, young spices overtake any hint of tobacco aroma. In maturity, this princely subject scales the heights of voluptuousness, exuding a magical Madera vapor.

Taste
All in the second act. Rich, thick, aromas subtly expand to spicy central tones, to finish in a symphony of brilliantly condensed bounty.

Enjoyment
One of the least known double coronas, the Gigantes is an unplundered treasure. Production is small-scale and reserved for the connoisseurs who swear by it. Perfect to savor after a fine dinner, with a splendidly aged vintage plum liqueur.

OVERALL RATING
Strength: 9 – Uniformity: 9 – Character: 10

Prominente - Cuba -

ROMEO Y JULIETA EXHIBICIÓN N°2
LIMITED EDITION

Length: 7⅝ in. (194 mm)
Ring Gauge: 49 (19.45 mm)
Body: square
Presentation: traditional box of 25

Look
An engineering feat by great architects, the double corona's *maduro* wrappers emphasize its long, virile "big cigar" allure. Looks that bespeak this cigar's potent richness, too demanding for some.

Touch
Full, sometimes to bursting, the body is so rich that it could be called oily. Consistently firm and supple, from foot to head.

Smell
Round, woodsy freshness, with the mix of rich scents that big players are known for. The unctuous backdrop presages a fine vintage.

Taste
Still in its callow youth (2000–2001) the Exhibición N°2 starts off with tangy touches, and quickly builds to stronger, still somewhat spiced flavor. The powerful finale can be a bit much. With maturation, this cigar should bestow the roundness of age on its richness, enhanced by a mellow hint of Madera.

Enjoyment
This unique cigar will be a collector's item, reaching robust maturity in five to seven years. It deserves to be smoked with the finest food, accompanied by a tannic, though mellowed Cabernet Sauvignon.

OVERALL RATING
Strength: 9½ – Uniformity: 8½ – Character: 9½

Prominente - Cuba -

VEGAS ROBAINA DON ALEJANDRO

Length: 7 5/8 in. (194 mm)
Ring Gauge: 49 (19.45 mm)
Body: square
Presentation: traditional box of 25

Look
Sumptuously cloaked, most often in *colorado* tones, and adorned with an elegant brown and gold ring, this double corona is as imposing as it is promising.

Touch
The supple body is so smoothly oiled, that it can leave a fine film on your fingers. The squared shape emphasizes the feeling of uniformity.

Smell
The generous bouquet, greener at the foot and more leathery in the body, foretells strong aroma. The finale is uniquely long-lasting, with a touch of green.

Taste
The harsh flavor when young has been known to turn away some potential admirers. With time, the Don Alejandro gains roundness, and its aggressive taste softens to smooth, deep flavors which retain a satisfying hint of raw freshness. The woodsy aromas become heady and intoxicating with smoking, to finish on mellow, melted tannic notes.

Enjoyment
With its outstanding style and taste, the Don Alejandro is a feather not only in the cap of the Vegas Robaina brand, but of the double corona format in general. Perfect for after dinner, in cool weather, after a continental repast with a fine, hardy Burgundy wine.

OVERALL RATING
Strength: 9 – Uniformity: 9 – Character: 9

Julieta - Cuba -

BOLÍVAR CORONAS GIGANTES CABINET SELECTION

Length: 7 in. (178 mm)
Ring Gauge: 47 (18.65 mm)
Body: round
Presentation: cabinet of 50; traditional box of 25

Look
This cigar's perfect appearance makes it stand out as a great among great churchills. Light or deeper brown in tone, the proud body is topped by an expertly rounded head.

Touch
This seductive heavyweight is robed in smooth and silky, lush wrappers. Supple yet tensed, this cigar should be kept away from dampness, which can soften it. Consistent, personal style.

Smell
The generous bouquet of earth and woodsy scents is never too spicy. This Bolivar's strength exemplifies the brand's tradition. Proper maturation releases its full, resonant force.

Taste
Rich and potent from the second third on, this highly consistent cigar makes each state of its taste evolution apparent to the bona fide smoker. Especially fine after a fish dinner with a heavier white wine.

Enjoyment
Long unavailable to the general public, this discreet cigar wins for its consistency. It makes a fine vintage. The cabinet selection of 50 is preferable to the traditional box for its superior bouquet.

OVERALL RATING
Strength: 8 – Uniformity: 7½ – Character: 8½

• In the same family, the **Sancho Panza Coronas Gigantes** is more earthy and milder.

Julieta - Cuba -

LA GLORIA CUBANA TAÍNOS

Length: 7 in. (178 mm)
Ring Gauge: 47 (18.65 mm)
Body: round
Presentation: traditional box of 10

Look
Open the box and the ten cigars are a pure work of art, ringed in gold and wrapped in deep, rich brown. The aromatic hints are borne out in the smoking.

Touch
Thick, supple, and taut. The Taínos can sometimes be a bit tightly wound at the head, but the body is consistently uniform. Fragile at the foot like all fine larger models, it is nonetheless well built, solid, and imposing.

Smell
The discreet, subtle aroma of well-oiled leather. The spicy notes, concentrated at the foot, bring out the woodsy, ambered character of the classic scent.

Taste
Rich and potent, the Taínos' flavor range is deep, round, and expansive, delivering sustained, substantial woodsy and spiced flavors in the mouth. The overall impression is exceptionally harmonious for this format.

Enjoyment
This truly grand cigar is especially fine when aged. Its one fault is synonymous with its greatest attribute: its uncommonness. For cigar connoisseurs, its complexity and consistency make a rare after-dinner treat. Unforgettable in the company of a fine, tannic Bordeaux wine.

OVERALL RATING
Strength: 8½ – Uniformity: 8 – Character: 8½

• In the same family, the **Partagás Churchills de Luxe** is less elegant in appearance and spicier in flavor.

Julieta - Cuba -

H. UPMANN SIR WINSTON

Length: 7 in. (178 mm)
Ring Gauge: 47 (18.65 mm)
Body: round
Presentation: semi-varnished box of 25

Look
The old, deep green box brought to mind a cask of precious emeralds. The new varnished wood casing is equally elegant. These majestic churchills range from pale honey to black chocolate in color. The range includes a sumptuous, uniquely intense *maduro* hue.

Touch
Crafted with only the finest wrapper leaves, the Sir Winston is both rugged and smooth to the touch, with an underlying silkiness.

Smell
Particularly woodsy and green at its youngest, the Sir Winston gains depth and thickness with age. The central note of dark cacao is highly developed, round, and imposing.

Taste
Impeccably potent and elegant, this great churchill generously deploys its spicy, strong aroma. Amber hints incise the flavor on your palate. This cigar is indisputably for true connoisseurs of the format.

Enjoyment
Made for great occasions, this indefatigable depth player will completely win you over. The occasional, slight imperfections are outweighed by the outstanding overall quality.

OVERALL RATING
Strength: 9 – Uniformity: 7½ – Character: 8½

• In the same family, the **Cohiba Esplendidos** allies class with panache.

Julieta - Cuba -

PUNCH CHURCHILLS

Length: 7 in. (178 mm)
Ring Gauge: 47 (18.65 mm)
Body: round
Presentation: cabinet of 50; traditional box of 25

Look
Less elegant but more ample than the Punch double corona, the Punch Churchills is a pedigree breed. The half wheel shows off a round of perfectly modeled heads. The color range tends towards dark brown, with an occasional, dazzling *claro*.

Touch
As usual for the Punch brand, unctuous richness and velvety texture win out over silkiness. More taut than pliable, the body is not short on suppleness.

Smell
At first highly vegetal, the aroma quickly develops in earthy tonalities of wet hay and rain-ploughed fields; scents that will move you inside. The body exudes the warmth of humid leather, underlined by a powdery dash of spice.

Taste
The young Punch Churchills is earthy, tannic, and thick, never dry or flat. With age, the flavor develops a fine woodsy range, heady and peppery. The vintage cigar's roundness perfectly melds all the registers.

Enjoyment
This cigar's richness makes it a rewarding after-dinner treat. Excellent with a fine rum: earthiness complementing woodsyness.

OVERALL RATING
Strength: 9½ – Uniformity: 8 – Character: 9

• In the same family, the **Romeo y Julieta Prince of Wales**, slightly less earthy, and more vegetal.

Julieta - Cuba -

QUAI D'ORSAY IMPERIALES

Length: 7 in. (178 mm)
Ring Gauge: 47 (18.65 mm)
Body: round
Presentation: unvarnished box of 25

Look
In its natural wood box, this handsome offering of golden rounds is almost never *maduro* in tone, and makes an indisputably noble impression.

Touch
Velvety, thick, and supple, but well-packed, especially at the head, which is slightly compact compared to the body. This well-crafted julieta is a joy in the hand.

Smell
Floral, delicate, and generous at the foot, the scent takes on a dry leather touch in the body. The overall light and aromatic effect makes for a classy, gentlemanly smoke.

Taste
From a mild, dry, chocolaty start, the second third unfolds richer floral flavor, generously aromatic. The burgeoning hints of musk and spices never overpower the dry base note. Easy combustion serves the overall equilibrium without ever tiring the palate.

Enjoyment
Consigned to the second string for years, this mild, fresh churchill has finally come into its own, satisfying lovers of the large, light and flavorful format. Fine in summer, following a light fish lunch.

OVERALL RATING
Strength: 6½ – Uniformity: 8½ – Character: 7½

• In the same family, the **Sancho Panza Coronas Gigantes** *is more vegetal and less aromatic.*

Julieta - Cuba -

EL REY DEL MUNDO TAÍNOS

Length: 7 in. (178 mm)
Ring Gauge: 47 (18.65 mm)
Body: round
Presentation: unvarnished box of 25

Look
This handsome churchill's fine, silky wrappers range from pale to deep in color. Though lovers of the brand show a preference for the *claro* tone, the *maduro claro* happens to suit it to a T.

Touch
Supple and firm at the same time, with a highly regular consistency. This cigar is smooth to the touch and feels just right in the hand.

Smell
The scent starts off subtly, then unfolds through woodsy, almost dry tonalities to expand into the light, fresh, round aromas of new leather.

Taste
This well-engineered churchill opens out in a mild, slow aromatic journey. The start is on the woodsy side, while the middle's poised, heavy tonalities rank this cigar among the grandees.

Enjoyment
With its reputation as the lightest of Cuban julietas, the El Rey del Mundo Taínos is often overshadowed by the format's star models. It deserves a place of honor among this fine family, and is ideal after lunch in the country or with champagne. The woodsy flavor is a great taste compliment to the freshness of an extra-brut champagne.

OVERALL RATING
Strength: 5 – Uniformity: 7 – Character: 7

• In the same family, the **Hoyo de Monterrey Churchills** is more consistent, yet mild.

Julieta - Cuba -

ROMEO Y JULIETA CHURCHILLS

Length: 7 in. (178 mm)
Ring Gauge: 47 (18.65 mm)
Body: square
Presentation: traditional box of 25, with or without aluminum tubes

Look
The traditional squared presentation (without the tube) comes in a wide range of hues, with deep *maduro* predominating. Good regularity, despite the veiny wrappers.

Touch
Inconsistent manufacturing runs the gamut from flaccid mushiness to over-packed. Ideally between the two extremes, this churchill is supple rather than soft, with finely oiled wrappers. The head is round and the body straight and erect, making it a pleasure in the hand.

Smell
After a highly floral outset, bolder, more horsy aromas of stables and leather take the lead. A greenish background note heralds a substantial cigar.

Taste
Despite the lamentably irregular quality, at its best, this mythic vitola deploys a fine, spiced aromatic palate. It is rustic and not round, but rich and strong into the last third. Though its finale is full force, the Romeo y Julieta Churchills burns balanced, easy and consistent.

Enjoyment
Perfect after a winter dinner, with an old Armagnac that adds to its great dimensionality.

OVERALL RATING
Strength: 9 – Uniformity: 6 – Character: 6½

Julieta - Cuba -

SAINT LUIS REY CHURCHILLS

Length: 7 in. (178 mm)
Ring Gauge: 47 (18.65 mm)
Body: round
Presentation: cabinet of 50; traditional box of 25

Look
In golden tones, never darker than *colorado,* this stylish cigar is a wonder of architectural consistency.

Touch
Supple and velvety, more silky than oily, slightly rough, this cigar is perfectly consistent and homogeneous from foot to head. Well-balanced, highly satisfying in the hand.

Smell
The full bouquet comes quickly to the fore, accented with woodsy, slightly spicy aromas on an unguent cacao backdrop. Essentially round, bold, and richly earthy. Precision interwoven with nobility.

Taste
Superior combustion deploys the unctuous aromas which become strong by the end of the first third. The tone is exotic and spicy, with a touch of dryness.

Enjoyment
Also available in a box of 25, the cabinet selection of 50 allows this fine blend to mature to perfection, releasing supremely refined honeyed and woodsy flavor. This churchill is ideal for slow savoring after a fine French, Italian, or Asian meal.

OVERALL RATING
Strength: 8 – Uniformity: 8 – Character: 9

• In the same family, the **H. Upmann Monarcas** *(with or without tubes) is well constructed and more earthy in flavor.*

Julieta - Cuba -

SAN CRISTÓBAL DE LA HABANA EL MORRO

Length: 7 in. (178 mm)
Ring Gauge: 47 (18.65 mm)
Body: square
Presentation: traditional box of 25

Look
With their resplendent *colorado* hues, these cigars are as tempting as the milk chocolate they bring to mind.

Touch
The El Morro is rich, thick, and noble to the touch, with a slight tendency to fullness. A generously proportioned cigar.

Smell
This full-bodied cigar hides behind an initially modest façade. Slightly spiced earthy tones develop into a core of moist underbrush. The completely moist aroma range explains the slow start.

Taste
The foot is a bit distant and light, while the second third is full and round, stopping just short of heavy. The ripe, earthy, slightly peppery flavor opens into a powerful finale.

Enjoyment
This recent brand, founded in 1999, has yet to win unanimous approval. A new line is always worth discovering, especially one that has variety on its side. The El Morro should take its place among lovers of rich, complex flavor, once its full potential is brought out with maturation. The vitolas are designed to accompany a great, full-blown Burgundy after a down-home meal.

OVERALL RATING
Strength: 7 – Uniformity: 8 – Character: 8½

Churchill - Dominican Republic -

MONTECRISTO CORONAS GRANDES

Length: 5¾ in. (146 mm)
Ring Gauge: 48 (19 mm)
Body: round
Presentation: traditional box of 25, individually cellophane wrapped

Look
This handsome cigar is wrapped in hues from golden yellow to light brown. The dark brown ring distinguishes it from Cuban Montecristos. The body's perfect roundness is prolonged in the head, making for an elegant whole.

Touch
At once supple and taut, this highly regular cigar is a joy in the hand.

Smell
Vegetal and woodsy at the foot, with a moist leather scent in the body. The short-lived aromas are delivered by a whiff of green characteristic of this type of blend.

Taste
An astonishing freshness, followed by a wonderful smoothness. The thick notes are almost absent, replaced by nicely rounded woody aroma. But beware, an overly quick draw could lead to unpleasant overheating.

Enjoyment
Perfect for newcomers to this format, the Coronas Grandes is fine for a before dinner drink, and will not ruin the taste buds or appetite for eating. The combustion is rhythmic and slow. This cigar is available only in the United States and the Dominican Republic.

OVERALL RATING
Strength: 6½ – Uniformity: 9 – Character: 8½

Corona Gorda - Cuba -

COHIBA SIGLO IV

Length: 5 ⅝ in. (143 mm)
Ring Gauge: 46 (18.26 mm)
Body: round
Presentation: traditional box of 25

Look
The mass is generous and the construction, majestic. Most often ranging gold to deep *maduro* in color, with a few *claro* or bright *colorado* exceptions, the Siglo IV has the silky elegance of a great, exceptionally balanced gran corona.

Touch
This velvety, lush cigar feels good in the hand. Grasped too tightly, it becomes difficult to draw smoke.

Smell
Overflowing with spicy and woody scents at the head, the aroma is much more vegetal at the foot, but the intensity continues.

Taste
The Siglo IV's richness and strength is typical of the Cohiba brand. Its potent, unctuous, round spice flavors remain into the last third, with exceptional generosity. Long in the mouth and well oiled, this cigar leaves a lasting impression on the palate.

Enjoyment
The competition is heavy among corona gorda, but the Siglo IV is definitely at the top of the heap. It has the advantage of uniqueness, and stands out among the others. Perfect after dinner with a fine Armagnac, this cigar is for experienced smokers who can appreciate the concentrated strength of its last third. It makes a fine vintage.

OVERALL RATING
Strength: 8 – Uniformity: 8½ – Character: 9

• In the same family, the **Bolívar Coronas Extra** is less refined, yet strong.

Corona Gorda - Cuba -

HOYO DE MONTERREY ÉPICURE N°1

Length: 5⅝ in. (143 mm)
Ring Gauge: 46 (18.26 mm)
Body: round
Presentation: cabinet of 50 or 25

Look
Though available in a 25-piece cabinet version, the half wheel presentation is stunning. The bundle's beauty speaks for itself, its tones ranging from gold to *maduro*, with a few light green variants along the way.

Touch
Perfect balance between diameter and size emphasizes the silky roundness, very fine to the touch. A grand model with imposing presence.

Smell
The Épicure N°1 is highly scented, in a consistent floral, thick range sometimes accented with the dry, greenish hint characteristic of floral cigars. The second wave is deeper, with rich cacao tonalities.

Taste
In keeping with the brand's venerable tradition, the first, highly vegetal puffs softly fade. It is only well into the second third that the developed, unctuous richness begins to meld with the woodsy aromas. The final third is slightly more concentrated.

Enjoyment
Like the N°2 (robusto), which has long been in favor, the Épicure N°1 deserves top billing. Perfect after a light summer meal with a fruity white wine or a less tannic red, the cigar is also fine after lunch, and will not tire the smoker out.

OVERALL RATING
Strength: 6 – Uniformity: 9 – Character: 8½

• *In the same family, the* **Punch-Punch de Luxe** *is similarly light, but more grassy and earthy.*

Corona Gorda - Cuba -

H. UPMANN MAGNUM 46

Length: 5⅝ in. (143 mm)
Ring Gauge: 46 (18.26 mm)
Body: round
Presentation: cabinet of 25

Look
A bundle of gran coronas in all its possible glory. Outstandingly crafted, with a rich chromatic range running from *claro* to *colorado*.

Touch
Packed yet highly supple, the Magnum 46 is a heavyweight, as you can tell from lifting the bundle. Particularly unctuous, silky yet not velvety, this cigar sometimes leaves a trace of oil behind on the waxed paper.

Smell
This noble beast exudes woodsy, delicately spiced scents, opening to a cacao core with deep notes of lightly tanned leather. The bouquet is irresistibly tempting.

Taste
After a slow start, the taste quickly builds to woodsy spices with an exotic accent. The finale is thick and round, almost heady. An atypical H. Upmann.

Enjoyment
This cigar's beauty is due above all to its superior homogeneity and consistency; no small order for such small scale production. Its limited availability is also part of its appeal among a handful of aficionados. Among corona gorda specialists the Magnum 46 is prized for its aromatic range. Ideal after dining on fish or fowl.

OVERALL RATING
Strength: 7 – Uniformity: 9 – Character: 9½

• In the same family, the **H. Upmann Super Coronas**, produced in a limited edition, is high in regularity and quality.

Corona Gorda - Cuba -

JUAN LÓPEZ SELECCIÓN N°1

Length: 5⅝ in. (143 mm)
Ring Gauge: 46 (18.26 mm)
Body: round
Presentation: cabinet of 25

Look
A bound bunch of Juan López N°1 exudes purity and integrity. The unringed wrappers are generally *claro* or *colorado claro;* occasionally *maduro* in hue. The round heads are exceptionally consistent.

Touch
More silky than oily in the hand, with a robust feel of suppleness and perfect porosity. The round head and foot are slightly firm without being compact. The no-nonsense texture is to the touch what the straightforward scent is to the smell.

Smell
Starting from the foot, the scents are direct, rich, round, and cacao-tinged. They develop in woodsy dimensionality on a leather backdrop for true aromatic fireworks.

Taste
Generous flavor from the start, with a mix of vegetal and earthy tastes. The last third releases woodsy flavors with a touch of moist spice.

Enjoyment
Indisputably among the crown jewels of the corona gorda, this superior cigar has the added plus of never tiring a smoker, thanks to a wonderfully effortless combustion, exceptional for the format. Perfect for exotic cuisine.

OVERALL RATING
Strength: 7½ – Uniformity: 8½ – Character: 9

Corona Gorda - Cuba -

PUNCH ROYAL SELECTION N°11

Length: 5⅝ in. (143 mm)
Ring Gauge: 46 (18.26 mm)
Body: round
Presentation: cabinet of 25

Look
The bundle presentation complements the fine construction of this young, elegant cigar. Colors range from very pale *claro* to a rich dark brown, by way of light green hues.

Touch
Supple and dense at the same time, this gran corona's wrapper is smooth to the touch. With its outstanding balance and perfect roundness, it feels good in the hand.

Smell
The highly floral, slightly thick bouquet is atypical for the Punch brand. The scent is intensified with a ripe vegetal tonality accented by an earthy hint.

Taste
The flavor sensation opens in an aromatic floral key: round, honeyed, congenial, and uncomplicated by spices. This expands in a highly original way to take on fresh earthy notes that balance the overall richness.

Enjoyment
This undeniably great Havana's flavorful complexity echoes its architectural simplicity. Inveterate admirers are thrilled to have it back in circulation after a long time off the market. Savor this great cigar after a meal of grilled sea bass with a fruity white wine, on a fine summer's eve, outdoors. Unforgettable.

OVERALL RATING
Strength: 7 – Uniformity: 9 – Character: 9½

Corona Gorda - Cuba -

PUNCH BLACK PRINCE

Length: 5⅝ in. (143 mm)
Ring Gauge: 46 (18.26 mm)
Body: square
Presentation: traditional box of 25

Look
The Black Prince sports darker hues, brown tones with fiery red nuances. The squared body, round head, and imposing ring are unmistakably virile.

Touch
Rough, leaving a filmy trace on the skin that is often an index of quality, this rival of the Punch-Punch is both supple and firm. Its fine proportion of size to diameter makes for a pleasant heft in the hand.

Smell
True to the Punch brand tradition, the start is earthy and slightly green. The aroma builds to spiced and leathery tonalities.

Taste
Heady. This truly grand corona shows its richness in the first third, mixing spicy flavors on a dry, woodsy background to bring out the strong overall taste. The bold, hardy sensation lingers long in the mouth.

Enjoyment
This cigar perfectly complements a dinner of game, offsetting rustic flavor with strong aroma. It is equally suited to highly spiced exotic cuisine. A cigar connoisseur's cigar.

OVERALL RATING
Strength: 9 – Uniformity: 9 – Character: 8½

• In the same family, the **Romeo y Julieta Exhibición N°3** is more vegetal and less strong.

Corona Gorda - Cuba -

PUNCH SUPER SELECTION N°2

Length: 5⅝ in. (143 mm)
Ring Gauge: 46 (18.26 mm)
Body: round
Presentation: cabinet of 50

Look
This wonder of a cigar often comes in *colorado claro*, and sometimes *maduro* hues. It looks even finer bound in the cabinet selection of 50. Avoid the matte green wrappers, which often encase lesser quality members of this lofty brotherhood.

Touch
The supple, responsive body is clad in velvety smooth wrappers. Pure harmony in the hand, thanks to balanced size to diameter proportions.

Smell
Woodsy underbrush on a summer's day after the rain: rich, round, almost intoxicating. The bouquet's earthy, moist thickness is deployed to its best advantage in the cabinet presentation.

Taste
A certain aromatic complexity and length in the mouth make themselves clear from the word go. Yet even the slowish start highlights this cigar's roundness and regularity. The second third unleashes a crescendo, leading to a heady, enraptured finale. The experience can prove too much for untrained palates.

Enjoyment
This elegant aristocrat shows its true colors alongside a fine arabica coffee, crowning a refined continental or exotic dining experience. The bold flavor is for experienced aficionados only.

OVERALL RATING
Strength: 8 – Uniformity: 8½ – Character: 8½

Corona Gorda - Cuba -

RAFAEL GONZÁLEZ
CORONAS EXTRA

Length: 5⅝ in. (143 mm)
Ring Gauge: 46 (18.26 mm)
Body: square
Presentation: traditional box of 25

Look
This supremely uniform, pedigree cigar struts its stuff in *claro* to *colorado* wrappers. Never quite oily, it exudes a silky, consistent, slightly austere elegance.

Touch
Rigor and rectitude from foot to head are the Coronas Extra's motto. Perfection through and through, in suppleness and density alike.

Smell
The highly aromatic scent recalls the Montecristos of the 1960s. Rich tonalities lend intensity to the woodsy core sheathed in floral notes. Enchanting.

Taste
The consistent, generous flavor builds in richness as it burns. Freshness expands with round, ample woodsy notes. This cigar never overheats or attacks the palate, but remains gentlemanly from start to finish.

Enjoyment
Although favored by many lovers of traditional Havanas, the Rafael González deserves an even greater measure of renown. Its small scale production may in part be the reason for its limited recognition. This cigar is excellent for after dinner or receptions, where its accessible side should bring it to the attention of a larger public.

OVERALL RATING
Strength: 7 – Uniformity: 8 – Character: 9

Corona Gorda - Cuba -

SAINT LUIS REY SÉRIE A

Length: 5⅝ in. (143 mm)
Ring Gauge: 46 (18.26 mm)
Body: round
Presentation: cabinet of 50, traditional box of 25

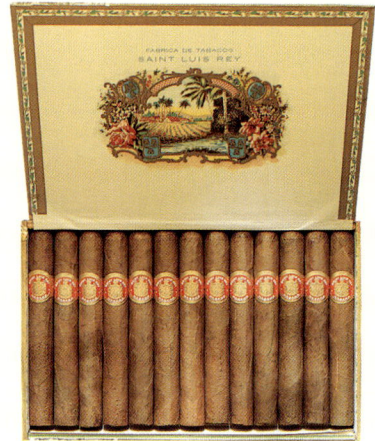

Look
The half wheel is perfect from foot to head, with exemplary roundness. The color range goes form *claro* to deep *maduro,* by way of green tones.

Touch
The lightly velvety wrapper binds a stunningly packed body. The fact that this special quality is only to be found in the cabinet selection, not in the box of 25, shows just how difficult it is to control the quality of a hand-crafted product.

Smell
The initial, seductive cacao scent opens into more floral vistas which, in the younger cigars, tends to fermented fragrance. The body exhales woodsy, dry aromas with a greenish character.

Taste
Rich, round and hardy, without excessive strength, this cigar is a feat of artistic flavoring. The start is on the light side, with a rounder, richer middle third marked by aromatic spices. The finale is full and generous.

Enjoyment
This handsome corona gorda fits well with today's preference for plenty of taste and presence without aggressivity. With its superior lasting power in the mouth, it makes a fine after-lunch or after-dinner smoke.

OVERALL RATING
Strength: 7½ – Uniformity: 8 – Character: 8½

Corona Gorda - Cuba -

SAN CRISTÓBAL DE LA HABANA
LA FUERZA

Length: 5⅝ in. (143 mm)
Ring Gauge: 46 (18.26 mm)
Body: square
Presentation: traditional box of 25

Look
This majestic gran corona resembles a double corona, minus the last third. Stouter than most of its brothers, it generally sports *colorado* coloring, never *maduro*.

Touch
Firm, thick, and at times just a hair short of too tightly packed, this cigar is no easy or quick smoke, despite its extra girth. The uniform construction, silky feel and generous proportions make for a pleasing heft in the hand.

Smell
Like the El Morro, the La Fuerza's first third is understated. It is not until you are into the second third that seductively round, woodsy aromas take over. Not to be confused with a churchill.

Taste
Highly satisfying when not overly packed, this cigar is initially herbaceous and fresh. It builds in subtlety, with classic woodsy, unctuous notes. The rich, tasty finale's fine longness will make you forgive the slow start.

Enjoyment
This talented new arrival should be given the benefit of time before passing judgement. It will be fascinating to compare the young cigars with their mature counterparts in a few years' time.

OVERALL RATING
Strength: 7 – Uniformity: 8½ – Character: 9

Hermoso N°4 - Cuba -

H. UPMANN CONNOISSEUR N°1

Length: 5 in. (127 mm)
Ring Gauge: 48 (19.05 mm)
Body: round
Presentation: cabinet of 25

Look
The 25-piece bundle tends to *colorado claro* tones. This finely engineered robusto is exceedingly uniform, challenging the Hoyo de Monterrey Épicure N°2 for top honors in its category.

Touch
The smooth, somewhat silky wrappers house a tensed, supple body, loosely packed; at times to the point of feebleness. A jewel of fine crafting.

Smell
A spring bouquet, highly floral and never heady. The generously oiled core brings beef broth to mind, at times with a touch of young, bracing leather. Fully present but never heavy or intoxicating, the scent is pure pleasantness.

Taste
Always light, never dull, the Connoisseur N°1 deploys a rich, unctuous aromatic range of exotically tweaked, woodsy flavor. The fresh start opens into a more fruity end. The overall fine construction never bogs down with time.

Enjoyment
This accessible, easy, companionable cigar has remained in the shadows far too long. It can be smoked at any time of day. Good maturation is sufficient; extensive aging does nothing to improve it.

OVERALL RATING
Strength: 6 – Uniformity: 9 – Character: 8½

• In the same family, the **Hoyo de Monterrey Épicure N°2** is an arch rival, and perfectly complementary.

Hermoso N°4 - Cuba -

EL REY DEL MUNDO
CABINET SELECCIÓN CHOIX SUPRÊME

Length: 5 in. (127 mm)
Ring Gauge: 48 (19.05 mm)
Body: round
Presentation: cabinet of 50, traditional box of 25

Look
This pale-colored robusto, nearly matte blond in tone, is similar to the Romeo y Julieta Exhibición N°4 and the Saint Luis Rey Regios.

Touch
At once silky and smooth, this cigar is the only one in its format to offer a perfect combination of consistency, suppleness, and flexibility.

Smell
The floral bouquet, with no spicy or harsh overtones, exudes a mild freshness uncommon in cigars.

Taste
The generous combustion deploys fresh, creamy notes accented with a salty taste on the lips. The smoothly uniform aromatic unfolding is never tiring. There is no doubt, it's a cigar with winning ways.

Enjoyment
The Choix Suprême has been around for more than forty years. After taking its time to make itself known, it is now recognized as an excellent smoke for a beginning Epicurean. Experienced aficionados enjoy the Choix Suprême in the morning, after lunch, or as a second evening cigar, when the taste buds start to tire.
This cigar is more complexly flavorful in the cabinet selection than in the 25-piece box. No long maturation is needed.

OVERALL RATING
Strength: 6 – Uniformity: 8 – Character: 8½

Hermoso N°4 - Cuba -

ROMEO Y JULIETA EXHIBICIÓN N°4 CABINET SELECCIÓN

Length: 5 in. (127 mm)
Ring Gauge: 48 (19.05 mm)
Body: round
Presentation: cabinet of 50, traditional box of 25

Look
This bundle of gold ranges from pale to gilded yellows. The perfectly rounded heads and feet and the body with a touch of paunch, speak for themselves with impressive uniformity.

Touch
The body is often on the softer side of supple, giving this pudgy fellow a fine porosity. The effect may surprise aficionados used to greater rigidity. Nice feel in the hand.

Smell
The fresh, highly floral, round bouquet is consistent from foot to body. The head gives off a subtle waft of green wood. Generous and modern.

Taste
Aromatic and ample from the first puff, with great freshness. Light, highly fragrant woodsy taste dominates the first third; earthy, grilled notes take over in the second. Even at full blast, the freshness holds its own, gaining in roundness. The finale is a tour de force of generosity.

Enjoyment
This temptingly spontaneous, accessible cigar is perfect after a light summer lunch, or with an afternoon chocolate treat in the mountains. Sit back and let the goodness sink in.

OVERALL RATING
Strength: 6½ – Uniformity: 7½ – Character: 8½

• *In the same family, the* **Vegas Robaina Famosos** *is equally tasty and nicely balanced.*

Hermoso N°4 - Cuba -

SAINT LUIS REY REGIOS

Length: 5 in. (127 mm)
Ring Gauge: 48 (19.05 mm)
Body: round
Presentation: cabinet of 50, traditional box of 25

Look
An aesthetic experience of roundness itself in the half wheel form. This handsome cigar sports *claro* or *colorado* wrappers.

Touch
The slightly thick texture is silky rather than oily. The supple yet taut body yields generously to the touch. Like all cigars with a slight bulge, the Regios feels great in the hand.

Smell
The initially floral bouquet develops into mild, round spiciness, with a green, vegetal hint.

Taste
The combustion is easy, but the vitola is tricky, and requires work before it yields full taste. The slightly harsh beginning notes quickly give way to more woodsy, round aromas, which maintain great freshness to the end.

Enjoyment
This robusto, abetted by the format's popularity in the 1980s, took its place alongside the Romeo y Julieta Exhibición N°4 and the H. Upmann Connoisseur N°1. It makes a fine after lunch smoke if you have an hour to spare.

OVERALL RATING
Strength: 7½ – Uniformity: 7 – Character: 8

Robusto - Dominican Republic -

ARTURO FUENTE FUENTE OPUS X PERFEXCIÓN ROBUSTOS

Length: 5⅛ in. (130 mm)
Ring Gauge: 48 (19 mm)
Body: round
Presentation: cabinet of 50, traditional box of 25

Look
This handsome robusto is clad in slightly shiny *maduro* tones. The round head, body and foot make for pleasing consistency.

Touch
The body is at once supple and taut, with no trace of over-packing. The slight oiliness bears witness to the cigar's richness. Its rounded body feels good in the hand.

Smell
The rich, peppery bouquet is dense and concentrated, in the ambered spice range. Fine, long-lasting scent.

Taste
The rich, imposing flavor starts off slightly dry in the mouth. Roundness comes to the fore in the second third, with unctuous, earthy, dry wood aroma, and a hint of wild game. The potent finale's round, heady force is delivered with excellent combustion.

Enjoyment
Ideal after rich dining, to bring out its affinities with heavy wine. This cigar is for lovers of strong taste sensations.

OVERALL RATING
Strength: 8 – Uniformity: 9 – Character: 8½

Robusto - Honduras -

FLOR DE COPÁN ROTHSCHILD 50
x 5

Length: 4⅞ in. (125 mm)
Ring Gauge: 48 (19 mm)
Body: round
Presentation: traditional box of 20, with individual cedar protection tubes

Look
A wonder of cigar artistry pokes out from beneath its cedar cloak, emphasized by a harmony of *colorado claro* tones. The oversized, modern ring, in red, white, black and gold, lends a rounded, jolly fellow feel.

Touch
Supple and smooth from foot to head, this cigar tempts the fingers with its slightly silky, never oily, allure. The loose packing makes for superior combustion.

Smell
The bouquet is brief and mild, with a great, unabashedly woodsy freshness. The highly mild, almost sweet aroma of the body expands to a floral register with an underbrush tinge.

Taste
A woodsy freshness is released from the first puff through to the end, never pressuring the palate. The flavor remains consistent throughout and does not linger.

Enjoyment
This well-crafted cigar is great for aficionados of heady flavor looking for an easy smoke, as well as for novices out to gain experience in the format. For connoisseur and beginner alike, it is at its best after a summer lunch.

OVERALL RATING
Strength: 6 – Uniformity: 9 – Character: 8½

• In the same family, the **Flor de Selva Robustos** is similarly constructed, also from Honduras, but differs in style and flavor.

Robusto - Dominican Republic -

VEGA FINA ROBUSTOS

Length: 4⅞ in. (125 mm)
Ring Gauge: 48 (19 mm)
Body: round
Presentation: traditional box of 25

Look
This slightly silky, highly uniform robusto wrapped in *colorado* is perfectly balanced. Its understated white ring bears the initials VF.

Touch
A well-proportioned cigar, it is supple on the outside, with a tantalizing inside. Nicely shaped, with the head's roundness echoing the body's bulge. A fine feel in the hand.

Smell
The mild, aromatic, fresh bouquet is slightly woodsy and short-lived in the nose.

Taste
Like all light structured, predominantly mild cigars, this robusto serves up a balance between taste and smoothness in the first third. A range of quickly fading, woodsy aromas comes out in the second third.

Enjoyment
The Vega Fina makes an enriching contribution to the taste range of the great Robusto family. This accessible cigar treats the palate to a slow, uniform unfolding of flavor that emphasizes the finale's richness. Never overtaxing on the taste buds, this vitola is perfect as an evening's second cigar. It is equally suited for daytime smoking at work, where the fresh, slightly dry aroma should not offend non-smokers.

OVERALL RATING
Strength: 6 – Uniformity: 8½ – Character: 7½

Robusto - Cuba -

BOLÍVAR ROYAL CORONAS

Length: 4⅞ in. (124 mm)
Ring Gauge: 50 (19.84 mm)
Body: square
Presentation: traditional box of 25

Look
This stout, squared-off fellow is instantly recognizable for its sharp angles and early-nineteenth-century ring. The highly consistent form is generally clad in warm *colorado* tones.

Touch
Slightly fleshy and rough to the touch, this robusto leaves behind the fine oily film that is a hallmark of rich, well made cigars.

Smell
An atypical Bolivar, more sweet-smelling and round than usual. The rather weak scent of the body is marked by leather, that of the foot is grassier and fresher. Both are quick to disappear.

Taste
Physical and present without heaviness, the taste is intensified by rapid, easy combustion. The highly woodsy start gives way to subtle spicy and savory tones. Harmonious and well balanced overall.

Enjoyment
Perfect for a light lunch or a moment's relaxation, the Royal Coronas is a favorite among aficionados who dislike excessive strongness. Have a glass of water on hand for the somewhat dry finale.

OVERALL RATING
Strength: 7 – Uniformity: 6½ – Character: 8

Robusto - Cuba -

COHIBA ROBUSTOS

Length: 4⅞ in. (124 mm)
Ring Gauge: 50 (19.84 mm)
Body: round
Presentation: varnished cabinet of 25

Look
With its golden or red earth tobacco, this robusto will stand out in any crowd. The Art Deco ring and the bulging form add to its overall appeal.

Touch
The bundle tempts the hand with rich, unctuous texture and hardy dimensionality. The outstanding suppleness lends elegance to this characteristically more rustic format.

Smell
The distinctive bouquet is generous and aromatic, rich in honeyed spices. Leathery notes, more marked at the head and foot, are borne on an oiled silkiness.

Taste
Rich and full from the start, the flavor blends spices and woodsy taste with great finesse. The ambered, fruity, honeyed notes increase through the final third with a seductive and winning alchemy.

Enjoyment
Despite complaints about its high cost, this brilliant robusto is undoubtedly the stuff of myth. Savor it after a generous dinner with full-bodied wines.

OVERALL RATING
Strength: 8 – Uniformity: 8½ – Character: 8

Robusto - Cuba -

JUAN LÓPEZ SELECCIÓN N°2

Length: 4⅞ in. (124 mm)
Ring Gauge: 50 (19.84 mm)
Body: round
Presentation: cabinet of 25

Look
Well-wrapped, at once silky and unctuous, this vitola packs old time "big cigar" allure. Though available in *claro* and *maduro,* it looks best clad in the red tones of *colorado.*

Touch
All around perfection: nice in the hand, thick and smooth to the touch, with a slight softness that becomes it.

Smell
The rich, intense start seems to belong to a very strong cigar, which this robusto is not. The vivid, chocolaty aroma when it's young rounds out into ripe, highly refined leather and pepper tones.

Taste
Easy combustion makes for rapid-fire unfolding of distinct flavor sensations. The pronouncedly vegetal start quickly expands into a half-earthy, half-woodsy register which never overloads the palate. Be careful of drawing too hard, which will cause overheating.

Enjoyment
This stunning Havana offers up a virtuoso aromatic panoply in the wink of an eye. You'll almost wish it could last longer. The Selección N°2 is fine after a meal, and equally good for daytime smoking, where its generous roundness is a real treat.

OVERALL RATING
Strength: 7 – Uniformity: 7½ – Character: 9

Robusto - Cuba -

MONTECRISTO ROBUSTOS LIMITED EDITION

Length: 4⅞ in. (124 mm)
Ring Gauge: 50 (19.84 mm)
Body: square
Presentation: traditional box of 25

Look
This handsome robusto sports two rings, the traditional Montecristo signet, and the limited edition band. It is distinctively robed in deep, lush *maduro* wrappers.

Touch
Like all cigars with deeply colored tobacco, the Robustos Limited Edition leaves a rich, oiled sensation in the hand. The richness is also related to the more than usually evident wrapper veins.

Smell
The strong, short-lived aroma exudes increasingly vegetal and spicy accents, on a gingerbread backdrop that bespeaks its young age.

Taste
Occasional combustion idiosyncrasies aside, this Montecristo wins points for a dynamic flavor atypical of the brand. With no tannic tones, the Robustos Limited Edition goes the spice route, offering a rich and strong aromatic range from the first third on.

Enjoyment
The Robustos Limited Edition was manufactured exclusively between 1999 and 2001. It perfectly embodies the era's cigar preferences, and is best after a hardy, strong meal with heavy, rich wine. Destined to become a great vintage.

OVERALL RATING
Strength: 9½ – Uniformity: 8½ – Character: 9

Robusto - Cuba -

PARTAGÁS SÉRIE D N°4

Length: 4⅞ in. (124 mm)
Ring Gauge: 50 (19.84 mm)
Body: round
Presentation: unvarnished box of 25

Look
High-strung and muscular, this tubby little aristocrat is most often elegantly wrapped in rich, unctuous *maduro*.

Touch
Pliant rather than supple, silky, and more packed at the foot than in the body.

Smell
A veritable spice rack, the bouquet is vigorous from the start, to the point of eliminating cigar newcomers. The round and unctuous notes on a slightly woodsy backdrop are accented with leather and green pepper touches.

Taste
Impeccable combustion delivers the full abundance of flavors, going from fresh to heady spices; from earthy to leathery and underbrush tones. The fast pace is never marred by excess heat. The savory complexity and intensity can overpower inexperienced smokers.

Enjoyment
After a time in the doghouse due to its poorly understood format and uncommon complexity, the D-4 has recently regained full honors. This cigar is truly exceptional in richness, consistency, and intoxicating density. It makes an unforgettable after-dinner smoke.

OVERALL RATING
Strength: 9 – Uniformity: 9½ – Character: 10

• In the same family, the **Montecristo Millennium 2000**, highly aromatic and expertly crafted, is already a collector's item.

Robusto - Cuba -

RAMÓN ALLONES
SPECIALLY SELECTED

Length: 4⅞ in. (124 mm)
Ring Gauge: 50 (19.84 mm)
Body: square
Presentation: traditional box of 25

Look
Lightly tanned, flat-bellied but round at the edges, this cigar bears the mark of determination. Amid the vast available color range, the slightly shiny red and dark brown tones are most becoming.

Touch
The firm body of this jovial vitola is tough, but not too hard. More oily to the touch than its relative the Partagás D-4.

Smell
Specially Selected's long-lasting aroma wafts spices on a cacao and caramel background. With proper aging, the honeyed core yields interwoven leather and rich spicy notes.

Taste
This authentic robusto is true to the great tradition, at once rigid and complex. Taste outweighs smell, with spices kicking in from the first puffs, mixed with round, unctuous, supremely sensual aromas.

Enjoyment
This Epicurean cigar is ideal with southwestern French food, such as fricassee, or long-stewed meats. Too short to go the distance of a great rum, it goes well with a fruity red Burgundy vintage that bears a trace of new wood flavor.

OVERALL RATING
Strength: 9 – Uniformity: 8½ – Character: 10

Robusto - Canary Islands -

S.T. DUPONT ROBUSTOS

Length: 4¾ in. (120 mm)
Ring Gauge: 48 (19mm)
Body: round
Presentation: varnished cabinet of 25, individually cellophane wrapped

Look
This handsome cigar's *maduro* hue is offset with a white and gold ring. The nicely rounded head and body are highly uniform, with wrappers free of visible veins.

Touch
A velvety feel emphasizes the rich, hardy, never too oily volume. The generous packing doesn't interfere with combustion.

Smell
The foot's freshness turns richer in the body, and slightly green for the finale. The concentration of aromatic freshness is mighty appealing.

Taste
This cigar's generous, nearly explosive combustion offers up aromas in rhythmic succession. The salted peanut start swiftly gives way to complex floral tones without missing a beat. Despite the accelerated draw, there is no overheating in the finale, making for short-lasting fine flavor.

Enjoyment
S.T. Dupont is the sole possessor of the secrets for making good cigars in Europe. This robusto can be savored in morning, afternoon, or with champagne before dinner. It leaves no after-taste. It also proves to be an excellent initiation to the format's complexity for novices.

OVERALL RATING
Strength: 5½ – Uniformity: 9 – Character: 8½

Dalia - Cuba -

BOLÍVAR INMENSAS

Length: 6⅝ in. (170 mm)
Ring Gauge: 43 (17.07 mm)
Body: square
Presentation: traditional box of 25

Look
The highly uniform, richly oiled wrappers come in a full color range, from the lightest *claro* to warm *maduro*, by way of a range of *colorado* tones. Green nuances are also possible.

Touch
Appearances can be deceptive. This seemingly stiff vitola is on the contrary supple, tender, silky, and lightly oily to the touch. It has an unmistakable elegance and feels so pleasing in the hand that you forget its squared form.

Smell
Like all Bolivars, Inmensas are chock full of spicy, earthy aromas. The slightly green underpinnings bring to mind the rustic scents of earth and farmland after the rain.

Taste
The subtle, woodsy start gives way to more complex, powerful underbrush and wet earth aromas with spicy, round notes and a touch of green pepper. The richly concentrated finale's unctuous flavor lends consummate balance to the whole.

Enjoyment
This extremely elegant, greatly generous, handsome cigar is still relatively unknown. The rich, potent flavor grows with each puff and draw of this smooth-burning cigar. Perfect after dinner for all experienced aficionados.

OVERALL RATING
Strength: 9 – Uniformity: 8½ – Character: 9

Dalia - Cuba -

COHIBA SIGLO V

Length: 6⅝ in. (170 mm)
Ring Gauge: 43 (17.07 mm)
Body: round
Presentation: varnished cabinet of 25

Look
With all the upright flare of a British colonial officer of old, this proud beauty is finely cloaked in rich, silky wrappers. To our knowledge, this is the only lonsdale-type cigar available in a cabinet of 25.

Touch
With its finely oiled texture, the Siglo V is as elegant to the touch as to the eye. A certain suppleness only adds to the appeal.

Smell
The generous bouquet is round and floral. The body exudes young leathery scents, while the foot is all mild spice and honeyed vegetal tones. The head breathes out the concentrated aroma typical of Havanas.

Taste
Aromatic richness comes to the fore from the start, in heavy floral tones. The complexly refined, spicy blend deepens in the second third, thanks to reliable, never over-heating combustion. The youngest of the bunch may be a bit tangy to the taste.

Enjoyment
This cigar is at its best aged: with proper maturation it is elegance incarnate. Perfect after a fine meal, or for an afternoon with a good book.

OVERALL RATING
Strength: 8 – Uniformity: 8½ – Character: 9

Dalia - Cuba -

LA GLORIA CUBANA MÉDAILLE D'OR N°2

Length: 6⅝ in. (170 mm)
Ring Gauge: 43 (17.07 mm)
Body: round
Presentation: semi-varnished box of 25

Look
This dalia mixes the material richness of a churchill with the lonsdale's elegant format. Generally golden but occasionally deep *colorado* in hue, with an elegant 8-9-8 presentation that brings to mind the Partagás 8-9-8 Varnished Cabinet Selection.

Touch
No softy, firm and highly structured, the Médaille d'Or N°2 sometimes borders on overpacking. The unctuous tobacco is refined and top quality.

Smell
The luscious, deep gingerbread aroma, more underbrush than unctuous in tone, sets this vitola apart from its Partagás 8-9-8 counterpart.

Taste
Strength mitigated with richness and presence. From the start, ripe woodsy and spiced flavor comes to the fore. This pedigree vitola then mounts to intoxicating heights, before delivering a punch with the finale.

Enjoyment
With its mix of unctuous mildness and potency, this fine cigar is the crowning jewel to an elegant dining experience. Its range may overpower inexperienced palates.

OVERALL RATING
Strength: 9 – Uniformity: 8 – Character: 8½

• In the same family, the aforementioned **Partagás 8-9-8 Varnished Cabinet Selection** is intoxicating. Ditto for the **Partagás de Partagás N°1**, with great classic strength.

Dalia - Cuba -

RAMON ALLONES 8-9-8 VARNISHED

Length: 6⅝ in. (170 mm)
Ring Gauge: 43 (17.07 mm)
Body: round
Presentation: semi-varnished box of 25

Look
This cigar's handsome, unified appearance is complemented by the varnished box. The overall effect is of a pleasingly rounded bunch atop perfectly aligned feet.

Touch
A mix of firmness and smoothness makes for a comfortable feel in the hand, reminiscent of a churchill.

Smell
Heavy spice and cocoa scents prevail in this rich, round, and extremely persistent aroma.

Taste
Cuban through and through, this cigar builds generously from an understated start. The unfolding gingerbread aromas will provide fine overall roundness with age. Careful: the highly packed tobacco can make for a vertiginously strong delivery.

Enjoyment
This eminent member of the prestigious 8-9-8 trilogy—in fine company with the Partagás 8-9-8 Varnished and La Gloria Cubana's Médaille d'Or N°2—is also the most unassuming. It makes an excellent after-dinner cigar; especially perfect following an Italian meal with fruity wine. For experienced smokers only.

OVERALL RATING
Strength: 8½ – Uniformity: 9 – Character: 9½

Cervantes - Cuba -

PARTAGÁS LONSDALES
CABINET SELECTION

Length: 6½ in. (165 mm)
Ring Gauge: 42 (16.67 mm)
Body: round
Presentation: cabinet of 50, traditional box of 25

Look
The cabinet selection's gorgeous half wheel is clad in golden tones of fiery earth that deepen with age. The heads are so well-rounded they seem closer to art than to reality.

Touch
The well-constructed cigar is firm to the point of being packed, and feels good in the hand. Finely wrapped and stylish, it is neither silky nor oily.

Smell
In young cigars, the scent is rather harsh and astringent. With time, this gives way to deeper, cacao aromas which build to the spicy strength Partagás are known for.

Taste
Ample woodsy and peppery flavor tantalizes the palate from the start. With smoking, the strong, woodsy character expands to grace each and every taste bud. The finale is a spiced medley.

Enjoyment
Beware: while the cigars improve with age in the cabinet selection, those in the boxed version seem to suffer from arrested development. At its best, this lonsdale goes hand in hand with great wines. Alternate between puffs and sips for an almost religious experience.

OVERALL RATING
Strength: 9 – Uniformity: 6 – Character: 8½

• In the same family, the **Saint Luis Rey Lonsdales Cabinet Selection** is stronger and less spiced.

Cervantes - Cuba -

RAFAEL GONZÁLEZ LONSDALES

Length: 6⅜ in. (165 mm)
Ring Gauge: 42 (16.67 mm)
Body: square
Presentation: traditional box of 25

Look
This great classic is perfectly elegant, elongated and well-built at once. The squared cut is highly becoming, especially in burnished gold tones.

Touch
Firm and packed, this cigar is a favorite among lovers of taut rigidity.

Smell
The nearly feminine bouquet, with its lovely floral notes, has no trace of spice. A green accent lends freshness.

Taste
The smooth, enchantingly subtle start opens into fresh aromas of mixed, delicate spices on a round, leathery backdrop from which continual unctuous intimations make you forget the slow combustion.

Enjoyment
This inspirational, imaginative, creative vitola goes well with a good book, or a musical interlude. It is fine food for thought.
The aromas never overpower the palate; on the contrary, they augment its discernment. Savor the cigar after a seafood meal, or following a delicious winter snack of cake and hot tea.

OVERALL RATING
Strength: 7½ – Uniformity: 8 – Character: 9

• In the same family, the **El Rey del Mundo Lonsdales** is milder.

Cervantes - Cuba -

SANCHO PANZA MOLINOS

Length: 6½ in. (165 mm)
Ring Gauge: 42 (16.67 mm)
Body: square
Presentation: traditional box of 25

Look
The box has changed, with jolly Sancho no longer pictured on the side. But the cigar remains its well-constructed self, available in a wide range of colors, and ringed with an elegant brown oval band.

Touch
Straight as an arrow, this cigar is nowadays packed to the point of rigidity, but retains a hint of suppleness when well executed. The slightly rough, grainy texture accentuates its austere allure.

Smell
Now the subtle bouquet is vegetal and green, without the interruption of any strong spices. This aromatic restructuring goes hand in hand with the new presentation.

Taste
The start is on light vegetal notes, with a touch of astringency. Only when it reaches the perfect temperature does the Molinos serve up its richer, more woodsy flavor. The intense last third may tend to overheat, due to its tight packing. It must be slowly savored, with pauses when it lags or races.

Enjoyment
Long-ignored, this cervantes has won praise for its richness and charm. Hopefully the new version will be equally pleasing, for example accompanying a meal served with a fine, tannic wine.

OVERALL RATING
Strength: 7 – Uniformity: 6½ – Character: 6½

• In the same family, the **Bolivar Lonsdales**, unlike the Molinos, makes a fine vintage.

Corona Grande - Cuba -

COHIBA SIGLO III

Length: 6⅛ in. (155 mm)
Ring Gauge: 42 (16.67 mm)
Body: round
Presentation: varnished cabinet of 25

Look
These handsome vitolas are well-structured, with uniformly round heads. Whether slightly longer looking in the cabinet presentation, or seemingly more abbreviated in the boxed version, the Siglo III is invariably appealing.

Touch
Consistent and packed without too much firmness, this cigar is elegant to the touch.

Smell
The first puffs release memories of fields, farms, and bucolic expanses, with the slightly heavy whiff of wet earth on summer mornings. The head is more leathery, while the body has a non-matte powdery aroma. The foot exudes floral notes mixed with a gingerbread scent.

Taste
Packed and therefore slow, this corona's first third heats the body to its perfect cruising speed. It then turns savory, quickly moving from dry notes to round spiciness. Proper aging transforms the strength into a uniquely delicate, honeyed richness.

Enjoyment
Few cigars in this format offer up such refinement. A few years after its creation, the Siglo III's impressive progress is to be admired.

OVERALL RATING
Strength: 7½ – Uniformity: 8 – Character: 9

• In the same family, the **Partagás 8-9-8 Cabinet Selection** (unvarnished) is more matte and long-lined.

Corona Grande - Cuba -

LA GLORIA CUBANA SABROSOS

Length: 6⅛ in. (155 mm)
Ring Gauge: 42 (16.67 mm)
Body: square
Presentation: traditional box of 25

Look
This impressively uniform gran corona, with its lonsdale airs, comes wrapped in hues from *claro* to *maduro,* by way of the red nuances of light *colorado*. The round head is artfully crafted.

Touch
Highly consistent, supple and sensitive but rarely too tight, the Sabrosos's classy looks are sustained by its fine quality tobacco.

Smell
The simple, direct, matter-of-fact bouquet speaks for authentic Havana tradition. Mild floral scents are borne on heavier, slightly pepper notes.

Taste
This classic iconoclast opens on refined aromas that quickly build in strength on rich, unctuous honeyed and pepper flavors. The good combustion assures a certain persistent freshness.

Enjoyment
Its top-quality tobacco, uniformity, and good value make the Sabrosos a cigar to be reckoned with. It is accessible even to inexperienced smokers.

OVERALL RATING
Strength: 7 – Uniformity: 8 – Character: 7

• In the same family, the **Romeo y Julieta Coronas Grandes** is more straightforward.

Corona Grande - Cuba -

HOYO DE MONTERREY
LE HOYO DES DIEUX

Length: 6⅛ in. (155 mm)
Ring Gauge: 42 (16.67 mm)
Body: round
Presentation: cabinet of 50 or 25

Look
With its beautiful half wheel of 50 presentation, preferable to the cabinet of 25 for extended aging, this cigar does not show its forty years. Its youthful complexion is gold toned, rarely darker, with a fine, silky texture.

Touch
At once supple and tensed, with a risk of tightness that makes it a bit hard sometimes, the Hoyo des Dieux is smooth, oiled, and silky to the touch. The bundle has a pleasing heft, and the cigar feels at home in the hand.

Smell
In keeping with Le Hoyo tradition, the bouquet is preponderantly floral, with persistent underbrush tones providing an element of variation.

Taste
The mild, round start expands with sweeter, deeper aromas in the second third. The finale brings out unctuous vegetal tonalities.

Enjoyment
Those looking for robusto-style bounty may consider this Hoyo a lightweight. However, it makes a lasting impression in the traditional taste range of cacao, wood, musk, and spices. The Hoyo des Dieux is fine after lunch with a young wine. Its balance and uniform, easy combustion also make it a good daytime choice.

OVERALL RATING
Strength: 7 – Uniformity: 8 – Character: 7½

Corona Grande - Cuba -

PUNCH SUPER SELECTION N°1

Length: 6⅛ in. (155 mm)
Ring Gauge: 42 (16.67 mm)
Body: round
Presentation: cabinet of 50

Look
The refined, attenuated look of this aesthete corona dressed in golden *claro* tones takes on lonsdale airs. Or is it the other way around?

Touch
The bundle gives an overall feel of mixed suppleness and tension. With its firm body and fine feel in the hand, the Selection N°1 is silky and smooth rather than oily. Its light packing gives it a look of confidence.

Smell
A mild cedar scent opens into cacao and leathery vegetal aromas in the body, and heavy, woodsy tones at the foot. While it makes an excellent vintage, time rounds, but does not alter the aromatic progression.

Taste
Less earthy than most Punch cigars, the Selection N°1 deploys a damp vegetal base in the first third, strengthening in the middle third with the rich, heavier, more spiced tonalities that mellow into a fine vintage.

Enjoyment
On the fence between two formats, this cigar has yet to gain a following. It is nevertheless one of the world's finest vitolas. Savor it after fine dining, or with an afternoon coffee, provided you have had a little something to eat first to mitigate the force.

OVERALL RATING
Strength: 8 – Uniformity: 9½ – Character: 9

• In the same family, the **Romeo y Julieta Coronas Grandes** is more floral and vegetal. It also makes a great vintage.

Corona - Cuba -

PARTAGÁS CORONAS CABINET SELECTION

Length: 5½ in. (142 mm)
Ring Gauge: 42 (16.67 mm)
Body: round
Presentation: cabinet of 50, traditional box of 25

Look
With the noble severity of a true corona, this handsome cigar dons generally gold colorings, with an occasional *maduro*.

Touch
Slightly velvety but not silky, thanks to the oils within. The firm body is supple but never soft, unless damaged by humidity, which proves its downfall.

Smell
The typically Partagás scent is a mix of woodsy and spicy, with a wild finale, especially in the young cigar. Maturation, especially in the cabinet, lends subtlety.

Taste
In keeping with Partagás tradition the Coronas Cabinet Selection has a certain strictness, with bold coffee, cacao, musk, and spiced aromas that start strong and last long.

Enjoyment
This handsome, somewhat austere cigar has built up a loyal following over the years. More fully developed in the cabinet version, its complex aromatic texture is the stuff of a superior vintage. Savored after an ordinary lunch, its slow, uniform combustion will never tire an experienced smoker.

OVERALL RATING
Strength: 9 – Uniformity: 9 – Character: 8½

• In the same family, the **Juan López Coronas** is equally strict, but milder and less spicy in the mouth.

Corona - Cuba -

RAMÓN ALLONES CORONAS CABINET SELECTION

Length: 5½ in. (142 mm)
Ring Gauge: 42 (16.67 mm)
Body: round
Presentation: cabinet of 50

Look
Long out of circulation, this coronas is back in a cabinet selection of 50, as if to show just how stunning a light-colored half wheel can be.

Touch
With its fine texture, silky and smooth to the touch, this cigar is firm yet supple. Well balanced from head to foot, its round form is pleasing in the hand.

Smell
The first wave is woodsy, with the aromas of woodland trails on a summer's day. This rapidly builds on honeyed, spiced notes which are unctuous and round in the foot, new leathery in the body, and ripened leather at the head. The generous aromas have both presence and persistence to their credit.

Taste
While the first third brings to mind a Partagas Corona, the Ramón Allones then gives off less spicy and fresher notes that are very seductive. The finale remains strong, offering rich, round, woody notes.

Enjoyment
This cigar's reappearance is cause for celebration, despite the snail's pace production. A tasty corona for the end of the day, a before dinner drink, or after dinner, its simplicity is winning.

OVERALL RATING
Strength: 8 – Uniformity: 9½ – Character: 9½

• *In the same family, the* **Hoyo de Monterrey Le Hoyo du Roi** *is slightly less rich in flavor, and the* **Saint Luis Rey Coronas**, *highly aromatic.*

Corona - Cuba -

ROMEO Y JULIETA CORONAS

Length: 5½ in. (142 mm)
Ring Gauge: 42 (16.67 mm)
Body: square
Presentation: traditional box of 25

Look
This great classic is all poise and pedigree, with perfectly balanced construction, a handsome traditional ring, and tonalities ranging from light to barely dark brown.

Touch
The supple, silky body is perfectly porous and bred to obey.

Smell
The bouquet sets out on a highly vegetal trail, then turns slightly acidulous, nearly sharp. The body brings out reassuringly traditional leathery notes, moving into a soothing finale.

Taste
True to its alluring self, not to preconceptions, this accessible, companionable corona serves up smooth and round floral flavor in keeping with today's tastes. Twenty years ago, this vitola was rich and strong, but changed to cultivate a following among lovers of smoother cigars with easy combustion that demands much less effort.

Enjoyment
This cigar's adaptation to current taste is a success story. ItÌ makes a fine friend at work for daytime smoking. Faithful followers will savor its fresh yet stable flavor anytime, anywhere.

OVERALL RATING
Strength: 6½ – Uniformity: 7 – Character: 7½

• In the same family, the **Diplomáticos N°3** is a traditional cigar that has made quite a comeback in recent years.

Corona - Cuba -

SANCHO PANZA CORONAS

Length: 5½ in. (142 mm)
Ring Gauge: 42 (16.67 mm)
Body: square
Presentation: traditional box of 25

Look
Uniform as a military parade, the handsomely squared body comes clad in hues running from *claro* to *colorado*. Its austere elegance is softened by the round head, and embellished by its brown oval ring.

Touch
Though slightly packed, this cigar is supple to the touch, and rigid on the palm. Its unctuous, slightly shiny wrapper lends a smooth, silky touch.

Smell
At the foot, the initial woodsy scent dissolves in vegetal nuances. The body exudes a hint of new leather that gives an overall appeal.

Taste
The first third is played in mild, floral tones, while the second takes a tannic, woodsy turn. The finale deploys rich, heavy underbrush aromas, with lime and coffee overtones.

Enjoyment
A great classic in the format, the Sancho Panza Coronas falls somewhere between Partagás richness and the Hoyo du Roi's mildness. Try it after lunch, without alcohol, to give its flavor your undivided attention.

OVERALL RATING
Strength: 6½ – Uniformity: 8 – Character: 7½

• In the same family, the **Juan López Coronas** and the **Punch Coronas** are admirably consistent.

Corona - Nicaragua -

PADRÓN 1964 ANNIVERSARY CORONAS

Length: 6 in. (150 mm)
Ring Gauge: 38 (15 mm)
Body: square
Presentation: semi-varnished box of 25

Look
Slightly longer than a classic corona, the highly balanced cigar makes a fine impression with its deep *maduro* wrapper.

Touch
Uniform, homogenous and loosely packed, this cigar is more soft than supple, with a bit of crackle inside. The slightly spongy texture encases rich, oily tobacco, for an overall moist feel.

Smell
The foot has all the aromatic mellowness of Indian tea, while the body exudes tobacco aromas in a vegetal underbrush base. Short-lived in the nose.

Taste
The highly floral, light, round aromatic range builds slowly to a slightly more flavorful finale. Avoid rushing the combustion to prevent overheating.

Enjoyment
This mix of tobacco, unheard of twenty years ago, has come into its own. The Padrón Coronas makes an excellent afternoon smoke, especially with an aromatic tea to hydrate the palate, which can dry out from its combustion.

OVERALL RATING
Strength: 5 – Uniformity: 7½ – Character: 7

Mareva - Cuba -

BOLÍVAR PETIT CORONAS CABINET SELECTION

Length: 5⅛ in. (129 mm)
Ring Gauge: 42 (16.67 mm)
Body: round
Presentation: cabinet of 50, traditional box of 25

Look
The bundle of round, well-made coronas is a gem of uniformity and consistency.

Touch
Smooth, firm, and taut, but never too tight, this cigar feels great in the hand. Hold the bundle to your ear; you can almost hear it breathe.

Smell
The alluring bouquet is round, fresh, and tonic. Wet-earth notes, initially subdued in the body, are more ample at the foot and head.

Taste
The earthy, slightly pungent first third builds almost to bitterness before yielding to mild spices in the last third. The overall impression is unctuous and consistent, with a fine balance between force and taste, long-lasting in the mouth.

Enjoyment
This petit corona cannot pack the complexity of a torpedo or churchill, but its aromatic range is one of the format's most fascinating. It goes well with a meal for the occasional aficionado, and makes a good daytime cigar for the experienced Havana lover. A strong little chap with indubitable taste.

OVERALL RATING
Strength: 6 – Uniformity: 7½ – Character: 8

• In the same family, the **Romeo y Julieta Petit Coronas** is more earthy than spicy.

Mareva - Cuba -

COHIBA SIGLO II

Length: 5⅛ in. (129 mm)
Ring Gauge: 42 (16.67 mm)
Body: round
Presentation: varnished cabinet of 25

Look
The homogeneous little bundle of 25 coronas ranges in hue from golden to deep red tones, with perfectly rounded heads.

Touch
Supremely silky, with an almost sponge-like touch, the firm, well-made cigar feels right in the hand.

Smell
The floral bouquet, with its leather and woodsy overtones, has an overall touch of pleasing moistness. Short-lived in the nose and devoid of spices, this cigar makes an excellent vintage, with pronounced Madera aromas highly divergent from its youthful incarnation.

Taste
The short and easy burn-time, no more than fifty minutes, offers up tastes in rapid succession. Floral notes give way to morning spices, then vegetal thickness. The second third builds gently to the finale's full array.

Enjoyment
Don't give in to the path of least resistance and smoke this cigar too quickly. Its rich aromas merit slower savoring. Tasty and structured, the Siglo II goes well with a simple meal, or finishes it off in style with an excellent arabica coffee.

OVERALL RATING
Strength: 7 – Uniformity: 8½ – Character: 7½

• *In the same family, the* **Juan López Petit Coronas** *is milder, with a squared body.*

Almuerzo - Cuba -

HOYO DE MONTERREY
LE HOYO DU PRINCE

Length: 5⅛ in. (130 mm)
Ring Gauge: 40 (15.87 mm)
Body: round
Presentation: cabinet of 25

Look
Understated, with no exterior signs of richness, the lovely bunch of petit coronas is a bundle of fine uniformity, in handsome golden tones, never too oily.

Touch
This thoroughly elegant cigar has a fine, silky texture. A bit overwhelming when packed too tight, and its slim shape sometimes feels lost in the hand.

Smell
The bouquet is mild, floral, understated, and short-lived. The body is vegetal in aroma, with no trace of bitterness or pushiness.

Taste
From its finely aromatic, slightly mild start, the smooth cigar gains richness and presence in the second third, before entering into full force for the finale, with green pepper flavor tinged with cacao tones. Some risk of overheating, an unpleasant result of tightness.

Enjoyment
This cigar is better in the company of food or drink than all alone. It can be enjoyed at any time of day, thanks to its easy combustion, and is particularly nice with an afternoon coffee or following a light lunch, on the way back to work.

OVERALL RATING
Strength: 6 – Uniformity: 6½ – Character: 6½

• *In the same family, the* **Sancho Panza Non Plus**, *a mareva, has a more matte flavor.*

Mareva - Cuba -

PARTAGÁS PETIT CORONAS CABINET SELECTION

Length: 5 1/8 in. (129 mm)
Ring Gauge: 42 (16.67 mm)
Body: round
Presentation: cabinet of 50, traditional box of 25

Look
The handsome half wheel of petit coronas, with their nicely rounded heads and feet, shows off the format's classic balance. The color range runs from deeper *claro* to light *colorado,* by way of ocher shades.

Touch
With no apparent oiliness, this cigar leaves a smooth, slightly grainy whisper in the hand. In the cabinet selection, this vitola is uniformly porous and supple from foot to head.

Smell
Fresh, vegetal, and short-lived. The young cigar's acidulous hints turn more woodsy, without forfeiting the vegetal base.

Taste
Generous from the first, the woodsy, slightly sugared aromas lend a special dimensionality. The bold, final third rekindles in spice. Aging merely hones its profile and mellows its style.

Enjoyment
This regal petit corona is straightforward, honest, and fits in everywhere, from a light lunch to a simple dinner topped with cognac, daily errands or a contemplative break therefrom. Provided you are acquainted with intoxicating Havanas, that is.

OVERALL RATING
Strength: 8½ – Uniformity: 9½ – Character: 9

• In the same family, the **H. Upmann N°4** is equally well-made and easy-going.

Mareva - Cuba -

POR LARRAÑAGA PETIT CORONAS CABINET SELECTION

Length: 5⅛ in. (129 mm)
Ring Gauge: 42 (16.67 mm)
Body: round
Presentation: cabinet of 50

Look
With the beauty of stripped down simplicity, this gold-toned petit corona has a hint of crusty country bread to it. The round head and feet and the harmonious body are mighty appealing.

Touch
Supple but not quite soft, this understated cigar feels fine in the hand. Its silky texture is smooth rather than oily, with more firmness in the body and head than at the foot.

Smell
The bouquet's enticing scent whets the appetite, starting with fresh floral notes on a slightly woodsy ground, and building to new leather tones in the body, with no hint of dryness or powder.

Taste
It deserves to be smoked young for its freshness, roundness, and tonicity. A slight fruitiness gives it a blithe tone that marks the beginning, while the last third is full of strong, abundant, lush aroma.

Enjoyment
This delicious petit corona is a well-kept secret worth discovering. It is highly adaptable, fine for daytime and after meals alike, and ideal for the gourmand who has no time or wish to dig into a bigger format, but relishes a flexible, ever-accessible smoke.

OVERALL RATING
Strength: 6½ – Uniformity: 9½ – Character: 9½

• In the same family, the **Diplomáticos N°4** has leathery aromas and a more squared style.

Mareva - Cuba -

PUNCH PETIT CORONAS

Length: 5⅛ in. (129 mm)
Ring Gauge: 42 (16.67 mm)
Body: round
Presentation: cabinet of 50, traditional box of 25
(Punch Petit Coronas del Punch)

Look
The compact, uniform bunch, with its greenish brown, slightly matte tones comes bound in a yellow ribbon.

Touch
More unctuous and smooth than silky, this supple vitola is somewhat crackling on the inside, but never dry, with a solid feel in the hand, unusual for this format.

Smell
Pure Punch. Earthy and moist, with a grassy vegetal foot in the young cigar. The body becomes more ambered, developed, and round with time. This cigar speaks loud and clear, with insistently rich, wet-earth aroma.

Taste
Superior combustion releases the ripe, earthy, nonspicy flavor with exponential impact. Honeyed, leather, and underbrush tones are equally present. The finale is strong and intense.

Enjoyment
Easy yet tasty, this cigar mixes well. For Punch aficionados, it comes in handy after a light dinner, and is also fine for work or a contemplative break.

OVERALL RATING
Strength: 8 – Uniformity: 9 – Character: 8½

Mareva - Cuba -

PUNCH ROYAL SELECTION N°12

Length: 5⅛ in. (129 mm)
Ring Gauge: 42 (16.67 mm)
Body: round
Presentation: cabinet of 25

Look
The compact bundle, with its gold to burnished tones, is elegance itself.

Touch
The bundle is a heavyweight for its format, with a nice heft in the hand. The packed, oiled body makes a fine overall impression.

Smell
The rich, wet-earth aroma, a signature of great Punch models, has a grassy touch that blends well with the body's soft leather notes. Depending on the year, this cigar may tend to show more acidulous, vegetal scents.

Taste
Real Punch, with a direct explosiveness in the mouth, the earthy flavor opens in a woodsy, spiced register, with cacao hints. The overall balance is winning.

Enjoyment
Despite its somewhat sluggish combustion due to density, this mareva is mighty pleasing. Passing irregularity is not to be confused with inconsistency here, where the touch of suspense only adds to the fun. With its generous roundness, the Royal Selection N°12 is nice after a light lunch or for afternoon smoking.

OVERALL RATING
Strength: 7 – Uniformity: 6½ – Character: 6½

• In the same family, the **H. Upmann Petit Coronas** is more classic, with a more linear taste range.

Mareva - Cuba -

RAFAEL GONZÁLEZ
PETIT CORONAS

Length: 5⅛ in. (129 mm)
Ring Gauge: 42 (16.67 mm)
Body: square
Presentation: traditional box of 25

Look
With its generally *maduro* tones blending with the ring color, this cigar's no-nonsense looks are emphasized by its rectilinear profile.

Touch
The thick, oiled tobacco is densely packed through and through, giving an edge of seriousness to the touch. The handsome, perfectly uniform wrapper is a fine result of the limited, painstaking production.

Smell
The highly vegetal start has a second wave of spiced aroma, which is typically short-lived in the nose.

Taste
The initial spiced flavors of wood and leather quickly build the peppery, tannic taste. Density has a hand in the rapid crescendo, which can border on overheating, and overpower an inexperienced palate.

Enjoyment
Not to be confused with the Petit Lonsdales of the same brand, which are excellent but less potent, this petit corona is perfect for European and American cuisine. It is equally fine with a before-dinner drink, at the end of the day, or as a second evening smoke.

OVERALL RATING

Strength: 8½ – Uniformity: 7 – Character: 7

• *In the same family, the* **Diplomáticos N°4** *is less strong; more floral.*

Mareva - Cuba -

RAMÓN ALLONES PETIT CORONAS

Length: 5⅛ in. (129 mm)
Ring Gauge: 42 (16.67 mm)
Body: square
Presentation: traditional box of 25

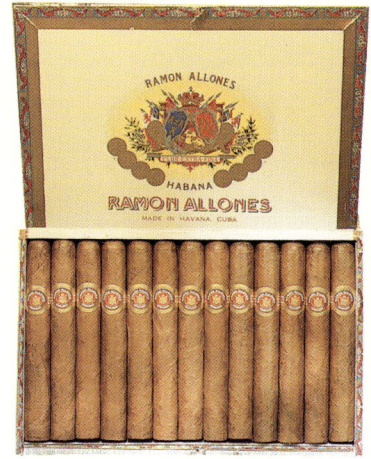

Look
This handsome cigar's *colorado* hues can spark reminiscences of Caribbean sunsets. The manufacturing and coloring is highly uniform, and the quality is definitely top drawer.

Touch
The highly consistent body is supple, taut, and perfectly porous beneath its rich, unctuous wrapper. Feels good in the hand.

Smell
The brusque, yet generous bouquet exudes rich and round leathery tones in the body. The foot is more complex, with irresistible individuality.

Taste
Oily, savory, rich and full. From the start, woodsy and ambered aromas build to the second third, which expands into a generous, gingerbread-tinged finale.

Enjoyment
Positive proof of the excellence this format has to offer, when only the finest ingredients are used. Better alongside rather than alone, the Ramón Allones Petit Coronas makes a great morning smoke for the experienced aficionado, or a late afternoon choice for beginners. For an unforgettable treat, try it with foie gras and a thick, strong not overly-sweet white wine.

OVERALL RATING
Strength: 6½ – Uniformity: 9½ – Character: 9½.

Mareva - Cuba -

SAINT LUIS REY PETIT CORONAS

Length: 5⅛ in. (129 mm)
Ring Gauge: 42 (16.67 mm)
Body: round
Presentation: cabinet of 50, traditional box of 25

Look
The beautiful half wheel shows off an oval of fifty petit coronas which are uniform, round, and silky, in burnished *claro* or occasional *maduro* tones. The perfect size to diameter proportions make for an exceptionally balanced feel.

Touch
This cigar is supple and porous throughout. The wrapper's fine, delicate texture is richly silky to the touch, lending an air of great distinction.

Smell
The round, fresh, woodsy bouquet gets off to a vegetal start, with a richer second third, mild and never spicy. The overall roundness is accented with a soft-spoken new leather backdrop.

Taste
A bit on the rustic side ten years back, today this cigar's flavor range is more complex, round, and aristocratic, with floral and woodsy notes.

Enjoyment
Formerly reserved for consummate experts only, this tasty Saint Luis Rey has won over less experienced smokers without sacrificing its character. The easy combustion, especially in the cabinet selection, makes this an excellent daytime cigar for connoisseurs, and is best with a meal for newer smokers.

OVERALL RATING
Strength: 7 – Uniformity: 8½ – Character: 8½

• *In the same family, the* **H. Upmann Petit Coronas** *is surprisingly round and mild.*

Minuto - Cuba -

PARTAGÁS SHORTS

Length: 4⅜ in. (110 mm)
Ring Gauge: 42 (16.67 mm)
Body: round
Presentation: cabinet of 50, traditional box of 25

Look
This brilliantly constructed, golden toned bundle, with its fine silky textures has the precision and alignment of a perfect log cabin. The cabinet selection is incomparable.

Touch
The unctuous, oiled body is pleasingly firm, with no risk of overheating in combustion.

Smell
The generous spring bouquet, at once fresh and round, builds along floral lines. A tiny leather hint brings out a touch of tannic character.

Taste
With an aromatic complexity unusual for this format, the Shorts delivers fresh, round vegetal flavor, mixed with spices and vanilla wood in the first third, and leather, honey, coffee, and more in the second. The bold finale is spicy. Long-lasting in the mouth.

Enjoyment
An excellent accompanist, this cigar is a perfect spokesman for the new millennium's taste requirements. It doesn't overwhelm the atmosphere, and takes just twenty minutes to smoke. It is equally good with a beer, coffee, light lunch, or a summer's afternoon spent outdoors.

OVERALL RATING
Strength: 8 – Uniformity: 9½ – Character: 9

- *In the same family, the **Diplomáticos N°5** is more squared and lighter in flavor.*

Minuto - Cuba -

RAMÓN ALLONES
SMALL CLUB CORONAS

Length: 4⅜ in. (110 mm)
Ring Gauge: 42 (16.67 mm)
Body: square
Presentation: traditional box of 25

Look
Though its shortness may keep it from standing up to be counted, the Small Club is to be admired for its superior uniformity and size to diameter proportions. This homogeneous cigar comes clad in consummate *colorado*.

Touch
The unctuous texture ranges from thick to grainy, depending on manufacturing. The ring size makes for a good feel in the hand. Aficionados who like to keep their cigar between their lips will like its fit in the mouth.

Smell
The short lived bouquet is no main selling point here. The slightly earthy, non-spicy scent is distinguished only by an understated, silky roundness.

Taste
The excellent burning quality lets the full and intense flavors show off their woodsy notes, which take on increasingly unctuous and exotic layerings that last in the mouth. Warning: the final burst of power may surprise you, but its impact is short-lived.

Enjoyment
This little format fits right between the index finger and thumb, to hide in the palm. The Small Club makes for easy smoking on all occasions, and is perfect to initiate occasional aficionados to the realms of greater aromatic complexity.

OVERALL RATING
Strength: 7 – Uniformity: 8 – Character: 8

• *In the same family, the* **Punch Petit Punch** *is a great representative of the new generation of small format cigars.*

Minuto - Cuba -

SAN CRISTÓBAL DE LA HABANA
EL PRÍNCIPE

Length: 4⅜ in. (110 mm)
Ring Gauge: 42 (16.67 mm)
Body: square
Presentation: traditional box of 25

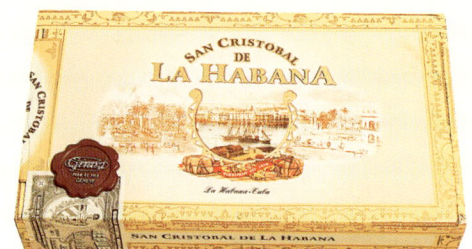

Look
With their candy-box presentation, these silky little *colorado* cigars have a winning air. The cigar seems to grow a bit once the large, somewhat odd, gothic-inspired ring is removed.

Touch
The highly supple El Príncipe is so manageable that it can get lost in the hand. Smooth, soft wrappers encase the oiled, squared off, pleasingly pliant body. Play with it a bit before lighting to enjoy the palpable moistness.

Smell
The body exudes a subtle floral, slightly woodsy, fresh scent. The overall effect is alluring but so short-lived that it has to be sniffed several times to really get it.

Taste
This modern cigar is easy, rapid, light, not spicy, and aromatic. It is suited for any moment of a busy day, delivering forty minutes' worth of unctuous, delicately woodsy, generous, intense flavor.

Enjoyment
If the first puffs don't quite pay off, once the flavor kicks in, you'll wish it would never end. This cigar's lightness makes it good for occasional smokers after dinner. It is also a fine morning choice for experienced aficionados.

OVERALL RATING
Strength: 5½ – Uniformity: 8 – Character: 8½

• *In the same family, the* **Romeo y Julieta Petit Princess** [4 in. (102 mm), ring gauge 40 (15.87 mm)]

Laguito N°1 - Cuba -

COHIBA LANCEROS

Length: 7½ in. (192 mm)
Ring Gauge: 38 (15.08 mm)
Body: round
Presentation: semi-varnished box of 25

Look
The elegant box opens on a jewel-like alignment of dignified cigars. The round foot, twisted head, and slim body exude 1960s style.

Touch
This aristocrat's silky texture and overall refined uniformity voluptuously stretch out in the palm of the hand.

Smell
Rich and strong in its heyday, the Lanceros is now more understated, nearly mild, in a vegetal, lightly floral morning register.

Taste
After a tiptoeing start, the second third is rich and physical. Cacao aromas, brought out with touches of licorice and spice, tickle the palate. Beware: defective fabrication can cause excess strength and overheating.

Enjoyment
A star of yesteryear, the Lanceros is unjustly forgotten today. When the fashion changes again, aficionados will rediscover its magnificent refinement. Feminine tastes may also help it out of its obscurity. An after-dinner cigar for the long evenings when time comes to a standstill and the philosopher in you comes out.

OVERALL RATING
Strength: 7½ – Uniformity: 8½ – Character: 7

• In the same family, the **Vegueros N°1** is consistently vegetal from end to end.

Laguito N°1 - Cuba -

TRINIDAD FUNDADORES

Length: 7½ in. (192 mm)
Ring Gauge: 38 (15.08 mm)
Body: round
Presentation: unvarnished box of 50 or 24

Look
Slender and spindled, with its head topped in a knot, this elegant cigar is handsomest young, before its *colorado* tones deepen. With time, the surface oils fade and the gold ring rusts to bronze.

Touch
Elegant and supple almost to the point of softness, the cigar is a joy in the hand, to be tasted on the palm before the palate.

Smell
Initially understated, the aroma unleashes woodsy floral body notes, with a mix of new leather. The foot is rich, savory, and lightly ambered.

Taste
Due to its size, the Fundadores starts slow and mild, building with heat to an impressive spiced range with a touch of pepper now and then. The subtle second third leads to an alluring finale that finishes off with slightly spicy notes.

Enjoyment
While most of the great brands concentrated on robustos in the 1990s, Trinidad focused on this unique format. The Fundadores makes an excellent vintage, and is perfect after a great meal with rich, deep wines.

OVERALL RATING
Strength: 8½ – Uniformity: 9 – Character: 9½

• In the same family, the **Partagás Série du Connoisseur N°1** starts off stronger and is spicier in aroma.

Delicado - Cuba -

LA GLORIA CUBANA MÉDAILLE D'OR N°1

Length: 7¼ in. (185 mm)
Ring Gauge: 36 (14.29 mm)
Body: round
Presentation: semi-varnished box of 25

Look
This gran panatela is a handsome long-line cigar, generally clad in *claro,* occasionally *maduro* hues.

Touch
More soft than supple, this cigar doesn't feel its size in the hand. The slightly unctuous tobacco leaves a fine film on the skin.

Smell
The alluringly generous bouquet's floral register is accented with a touch of gingerbread; a La Gloria Cubana hallmark.

Taste
Spicy, honeyed flavor builds body in the second third to deliver a rich, concentrated finale. Careful maturation lends unexpected smoothness and roundness, played out in a slow, round, woodsy rhythm that never dulls.

Enjoyment
The Médaille d'Or N°1 doesn't have the following it deserves. But it does number some ardent admirers, especially among vintage lovers, who revel in the discovery of its new aromatic horizons. With its sometimes energetic last third, this cigar is for experienced palates only. The combustion is highly satisfactory for this format.

OVERALL RATING
Strength: 6½ – Uniformity: 9 – Character: 8½

Panetela Larga - Cuba -

LA GLORIA CUBANA MÉDAILLE D'OR N°3

Length: 6⅞ in. (175 mm)
Ring Gauge: 28 (11.11 mm)
Body: round
Presentation: semi-varnished box of 25

Look
With their 1970s silhouette that makes them a darling of this format's connoisseurs, these three rows of long, finely crafted chopsticks are elegance itself.

Touch
This soft cigar eschews firmness and rigidity. Its round form slides easily between the fingers and feels natural in the hand.

Smell
The floral bouquet is fresh, unctuous, and unassuming.

Taste
This understated panetela is one of the format's most aromatic, yielding pleasing spice and honeyed flavor. The regular draw is an added attraction. The light, almost distant first third builds to rich woodsy taste in the middle third. Beware of overheating towards the end.

Enjoyment
While true to the finest La Gloria Cubana tradition, the Médaille d'Or N°3 is atypical for its format. Its easy combustion makes it perfect for a coffee break or a reflective moment. This cigar never over-saturates, but is a bit heavy and bold for beginners.

OVERALL RATING
Strength: 5½ – Uniformity: 7 – Character: 6½

• In the same family, the **El Rey del Mundo Elegantes** is popular among lovers of lightly flavored gran panetelas.

Panetela Larga - Cuba -

RAFAEL GONZÁLEZ
SLENDERELLAS

Length: 6⅞ in. (175 mm)
Ring Gauge: 28 (11.11 mm)
Body: round
Presentation: traditional box of 25

Look
With its chocolate cigarette looks, this fine, round, slender cigar seems to go on forever. It is clad in a color range running from the palest *clarisimo* to dark, warm *colorado*.

Touch
Packed sometimes to the point of rigidity, the cigar is generally both firm and supple. Depending on the tobacco, the texture runs from silky to slightly grainy.

Smell
A vegetal, subtly camphor scent pervades the body, while the foot is mild and dry. The overall impression is fresh and lively.

Taste
Exceptional combustion serves up a range of delicate woodsy aromas, never harsh or spicy. This light, accessible, harmonious cigar will not tire you out.

Enjoyment
The Slenderellas cigar is a treat for a luxurious morning or a stolen moment. It is a favorite among female connoisseurs, and may gain more of a following when fashion swings back to the elegant, less potent format.

OVERALL RATING
Strength: 5 – Uniformity: 8 – Character: 7

Anton Molnar, *A Letter*.

INDEX

Cigars of which names are written in italics do not have a page devoted to them in this book, but are referred to in relation to another cigar.

Arturo Fuente Fuente Opus X Perfexción Robustos 50
Arturo Fuente Hemingway Reserva Especial Signature 15
Bolívar Belicosos Finos 13
Bolívar Coronas Extra 36
Bolívar Coronas Gigantes Cabinet Selection 26
Bolívar Inmensas 60
Bolívar Lonsdales 67
Bolívar Petit Coronas Cabinet Selection 76
Bolívar Royal Coronas 53
Cohiba Espléndidos 28
Cohiba Lanceros 89
Cohiba Millennium 2000 6
Cohiba Robustos 54
Cohiba Siglo II 77
Cohiba Siglo III 68
Cohiba Siglo IV 36
Cohiba Siglo V 61
Cuaba Exclusivos 17
Diplomáticos N°2 7
Diplomáticos N°3 73
Diplomáticos N°4 80, 83
Diplomáticos N°5 86
El Rey del Mundo Cabinet Selección Choix Suprême 47
El Rey del Mundo Elegantes 92
El Rey del Mundo Lonsdales 66
El Rey del Mundo Taínos 31
Flor de Copán Rothschild 50 x 5 51
Flor de Selva Robustos 51
H. Upmann Connoisseur N°1 46
H. Upmann Magnum 46 38
H. Upmann Monarcas 33
H. Upmann N°1 64
H. Upmann N°2 8
H. Upmann N°4 79
H. Upmann Petit Coronas 85
H. Upmann Sir Winston 28
H. Upmann Super Coronas 38
Hoyo de Monterrey Churchills 31
Hoyo de Monterrey Double Coronas 20

Hoyo de Monterrey Épicure N°1 37
Hoyo de Monterrey Épicure N°2 46
Hoyo de Monterrey Le Hoyo des Dieux 69
Hoyo de Monterrey Le Hoyo du Prince 78
Hoyo de Monterrey Le Hoyo du Roi 72
Hoyo de Monterrey Particulares Limited Edition 18
Juan López Coronas 74
Juan López Petit Coronas 77
Juan López Selección N°1 39
Juan López Selección N°2 55
La Gloria Cubana Médaille d'Or N°1 91
La Gloria Cubana Médaille d'Or N°2 62
La Gloria Cubana Médaille d'Or N°3 92
La Gloria Cubana Sabrosos 64
La Gloria Cubana Taínos 27
Montecristo "A" 19
Montecristo Coronas Grandes 35
Montecristo Millennium 2000 57
Montecristo N°1 64
Montecristo N°2 9
Montecristo Robustos Limited Edition 56
Padrón 1964 Anniversary Coronas 75
Partagás 8-9-8 Cabinet Selection Unvarnished 67
Partagás 8-9-8 Cabinet Selection Varnished 62
Partagás Churchills de Luxe 27
Partagás Coronas Cabinet Selection 71
Partagás de Partagás N°1 62
Partagás Lonsdales Cabinet Selection 65
Partagás Lusitanias 21
Partagás Petit Coronas Cabinet Selection 79

Partagás Pirámides Limited Edition 10
Partagás Presidentes 17
Partagás Série D N°4 57
Partagás Série du Connaisseur N°1 90
Partagás Shorts 86
Por Larrañaga Petit Coronas Cabinet Selection 80
Punch Black Prince 41
Punch Churchills 29
Punch Coronas 74
Punch Double Coronas 22
Punch Petit Coronas 81
Punch Petit Punch 87
Punch-Punch de Luxe 37
Punch Royal Selection N°11 40
Punch Royal Selection N°12 82
Punch Super Selection N°1 70
Punch Super Selection N°2 42
Quai d'Orsay Imperiales 30
Rafael González Coronas Extra 43
Rafael González Lonsdales 66
Rafael González Petit Coronas 83
Rafael González Slenderellas 93
Ramón Allones 8-9-8 Cabinet Selection Varnished 63
Ramón Allones Coronas Cabinet Selection 72
Ramón Allones Gigantes 23
Ramón Allones Petit Coronas 84
Ramón Allones Small Club Coronas 87
Ramón Allones Specially Selected 58
Romeo y Julieta Belicosos 14
Romeo y Julieta Churchills 32
Romeo y Julieta Coronas 73
Romeo y Julieta Coronas Grandes 64
Romeo y Julieta Exhibición N°2 24
Romeo y Julieta Exhibición N°3 41

Romeo y Julieta Exhibición N°4 Cabinet Selección 48
Romeo y Julieta Petit Coronas 76
Romeo y Julieta Petit Princess 88
Romeo y Julieta Prince of Wales 29
S.T. Dupont Robustos 59
Saint Luis Rey Churchills 33
Saint Luis Rey Coronas 72
Saint Luis Rey Lonsdales Cabinet Selection 65
Saint Luis Rey Petit Coronas 85
Saint Luis Rey Prominente 22
Saint Luis Rey Regios 49
Saint Luis Rey Série A 44
San Cristóbal de La Habana El Morro 34
San Cristóbal de La Habana El Príncipe 88
San Cristóbal de La Habana La Fuerza 45
San Cristóbal de La Habana La Punta 11
Sancho Panza Belicosos 13
Sancho Panza Coronas 74
Sancho Panza Coronas Gigantes 26, 30
Sancho Panza Molinos 67
Sancho Panza Non Plus 78
Sancho Panza Sanchos 18
Santa Damiana Torpedo 16
Trinidad Fundadores 90
Vega Fina Pirámides 16
Vega Fina Robustos 52
Vegas Robaina Don Alejandro 25
Vegas Robaina Famosos 48
Vegas Robaina Únicos 12
Vegueros N°1 89

Acknowledgments

To Anton Molnar and Antoni Vives Fierro,
for having introduced art into the world of the cigar.
To my mother, for her example
To my wife, for her patience
To my sister, for her complicity
To Sévan and Taline, of course.

Translated from the French by Chet Weiner and Stacy Doris
Copy edited by Christine Schultz-Touge
Box set presentation an original design by Open Door, UK
Originally published as *Le Cigare* © Flammarion S.A. 2001
English-language edition © Flammarion USA Inc. 2002
ISBN: 2-0801-0721-6
FA0721-02-II
Dépôt légal: 4/2002
Printed and bound in Spain

Boutique Noga Hilton – 19, quai du Mont-Blanc – 1201 Geneva
Tel. + 41 22 908 35 35
Fax + 41 22 908 35 30
www.gerard-pere-et-fils.com
www.gerard.ch
info@gerard-pere-et-fils.com
info@gerard.ch

PÈRE ET FILS

THE ART OF CIGARS

PHOTOGRAPHS BY MATTHIEU PRIER

Flammarion

Antoni Vives Fierro. *Smoking Tobacco*. Oil on canvas.

CONTENTS

Preface	5
The Cigar, an Epic Saga	6
Cigar Country – Cuba	8
Cigar Country – Vuelta Abajo	10
Cigar Country – The Dominican Republic	12
Cigar Country – Honduras	14
Cigar Country – Nicaragua	16
More Cigar Countries – 1	18
(Mexico, Costa Rica, Ecuador, Jamaica, Brazil)	
More Cigar Countries – 2	20
(United States, Canary Islands, Indonesia, Philippines, Cameroon)	
Tobacco Culture: from Seed to the Casa de Tabaco	22
Fabrication: the Torcedor's Art	24
Galeras: Tobacco to Cigar	26
Quality Control	28
Cigar Architecture	30
Large Models	32
Medium-Sized Models	34
Small Models	36
Colors	38
Boxes and Cabinets	40
Vistas, Past and Present	42
Cigar Rings, Past and Present	44
Moisture and Preservation	46
The Humidor: from Wood to Altuglas	48
Ageing	50
Clipping and Lighting Up	52
The Art of Savoring a Cigar	54
Body and Flavor	56
Accessories	58
When the Time is Right	60
Middle Eastern Cuisine	62
Cigars and Alcohol	64
Cigar Speculation	66
Counterfeits from Cuba	68
Great Cuban Cigars, Past and Present	70
Vintage and Legendary Cigars	74
Collectors and Collections	76
Gérard Père et Fils' Special Blend	78
Latest Trends	80
The Cigar Smoker's Pantheon	82
Cigars Du Jour – Level 1 (Novice)	84
Cigars Du Jour – Level 2 (Amateur)	86
Cigars Du Jour – Level 3 (Aficionado)	88
Cigars Du Jour – Level 4 (Connoisseur)	90
Glossary of Cigar Terms	92
Index	94

To my father, who handed down the passion.

PREFACE

The richly varied realm of the cigar has but one constant: passion for excellent taste. This is the source of the cigar connoisseur's inspiration, the aficionado's motivation, and the *veguero's* watchword.

Cigars are first of all products of the earth, albeit one of the most noble and complex. Without the acumen, experience and know-how of the men and women who raise tobacco and turn it into cigars; without their assiduous expertise, cigars could not attain their aura and fascination.

A cigar's symphony of aromas and its miraculous harmony of flavors result from precise, patient, and intense work. Every stage of creation requires skill as well as exacting professional standards.

The members of the Gérard family are lifelong cigar lovers, and for a long time we would accept only Havana cigars. But the world has changed, and gone is the universe where Havana ruled alone. This book marks the culmination of years of rigorous research. The whole world of cigar production and connoisseurship is taken into account.

Despite upheavals and changes, including the disappearance and rebirth of some cigars, we can assure you that our vitolas are fit for the palates of kings. They are also available for all to savor with joy and gusto. We rejoice in the appearance of more and more aficionados with ever greater connoisseurship. This book is written for such champions of taste and delectation.

Vahé Gérard

THE CIGAR, AN EPIC SAGA

Mythic Beginnings of Tobacco Use
The indigenous Taino tribes of Cuba were the first to use what they called the *cohiba* plant during ceremonial rituals. After being dried and woven it was called *tabacco*, and passed from person to person, smoked in pipes.

In 1492, Columbus and his crew were the first Europeans to encounter the plant. Spain and Portugal were the first countries to deal tobacco to the rest of Europe, which would soon follow suit. At first tobacco was used medicinally, particularly as a purgative, a calmative, or a decongestive remedy. It was consumed by sniffing, inhalation, or after brewing. In the sixteenth century, Jean Nicot, a French Consul and the person after whom nicotine was named, recommended tobacco to Catherine de Medici, who used it as a remedy for her migraine headaches.

From Hand-Crafting to Organized Commerce
Europeans, mainly French and British, began organized cultivation of tobacco in the sixteenth century. They used slave labor on plantations in North America, the West Indies, and Cuba. Commercialization of the "amazing plant" spread to Malta, Italy, and the Netherlands, after which Turkey, Morocco and even Japan took up cultivation on a large scale.

England once again was essential in the history of tobacco consumption. It became so popular in Queen Elizabeth I's court that tobacco smoking spread from the aristocracy and sailors, who were its initial smokers, to other classes of people as well. Even the ladies in waiting took it up, in recognition of Sir Walter Raleigh, the queen's lover. Growers in Virginia, North Carolina, Maryland, and Kentucky became specialists in tobacco cultivation. And in seventeenth-century France, the first commercial import tax was levied on tobacco.

Above: Certain brands that were once the glory of Cuba have disappeared, among them La Corona (now only machine made), La Escepción, and Maria Guerrero.

Facing page: The Smoker, an Aztec engraving uncovered on the archeological site at Palenque, Mexico.

From New World to Old World, and Back

Carl Linnaeus was the first to use the term *Nicotiana tabacum*, in 1739. But it was Nicholas Vauquelin who discovered and isolated nicotine in 1809. When Napoleon's armies had overrun Spain two years earlier, they had discovered the *puro*, the first pure tobacco ancestor of the cigar, and helped spread the taste for it over the continent.

While Spain's *puros* first captivated European smokers on a large scale, and emulation of dapper English smokers assured its popularity through the nineteenth century, the cigar's glory days arrived in the twentieth century.

The combination of improved manufacturing standards in cigar design and appearance, cigar boxes, and the advent of cigar rings led to the cigar's reputation as an object of refinement and indulgence. Tobacco rolling was no longer done on the Iberian peninsula. And since tobacco traveled poorly, the best cigars, like excellent wines bottled at the vintner, began to be manufactured on the tobacco-growing islands. The result was a tremendous improvement in quality. The 1940s and 1950s saw the birth of cigar brands that are world famous today. Following their initial success, these brands diversified, introducing a variety of models and sizes.

Considered merely a trend at first, in the 1990s, the cigar captivated a large following of younger, more varied, and often highly discerning smokers in the United States and then elsewhere. Cigars began to appear frequently in books and movies, becoming almost a symbol of a certain sophisticated lifestyle.

This brought about the expansion of the cigar market, with decreased quality in some sectors and an amazing jump in prices. But taste also evolved—and continues to do so— in relation to the number of consumers, the degree of knowledge about the product, and lifestyle choices. All this is simply proof, as if any were needed, of the consistent yet evolving interest in the cigar.

CIGAR COUNTRY - Cuba -

Cuba is still the promised land for the cigar lover. Other regions have achieved the production of high quality cigars, but the stuff that dreams are made of is still found on the 153,200 acres (62,000 hectares) of tobacco fields located between the Gulf of Mexico, the Atlantic Ocean, and the Caribbean Sea.

The Great Brands
Production of Cuban cigars began in the first half of the seventeenth century. In the beginning it was confined to very small scale, even personal, enterprises. Exportation increased slowly, with the development of maritime transportation.

The real start can be dated to 1827 when the Partágas cigar and the first *fábrica* (factory) were born. Among other developments were the arrival of Larrañaga (1834), Punch (1840), H. Upmann (1844), Ramón Allones (1845), Sancho Panza (1848), Hoyo de Monterrey (1865), Romeo y Julieta (1875), El Rey del Mundo (1882), and Montecristo—which first appeared in 1935. Quality control at every stage of production was assured, and the Cuban cigar spread its taste empire throughout the world.

The Revolution
Fidel Castro's ascension to power on January 2, 1959 brought unprecedented economic difficulties. Castro was determined to apply Marxist principles in every domain of the economy, and thus decreed the nationalization of means of cigar production and the abolition of brands. International repercussions led to the drastic free fall of exports. In the face of this disaster Castro retracted somewhat. Lands were restored to farmers and models and brands of cigar were revived. But it was not until the middle of the 1960s that Cuban cigars regained their prestige and quality. Now yearly output of cigars in Cuba amounts to nearly 350 million, of which 150 million are *totalmente hecho a mano* (exclusively handmade).

Cuba's Five Great Regions
Like fine wine, tobaccos from different regions each have their own special qualities. Moving from east to west, Cuba's five great regions are:

HABANA

- **Vuelta Abajo**. This is the best region of all. Without a doubt the best tobacco in the world comes from its 79,035 acres (32,000 hectares).

- **Semi-Vuelta**. Although it is also located on the west of the island, tobaccos from this region cannot be compared to those of Vuelta-Abajo. Semi-Vuelta tobacco is mainly used for cigarettes.

- **Partido**. This "land of the pale wrapper" is located near Havana. Tobacco leaves from here produce lighter-colored leaves sometimes used as wrappers—to the chagrin of some cigar traditionalists.

- **Remedios** This is a newly discovered land for most cigar smokers. It is located in the center of the island, and until recently Remedios tobacco was kept exclusively for the domestic market. Recently the Cuban cigar authorities have been making large scale efforts at improving quality and reaching out to international markets, calling the tobacco Vuelta Arriba. These attempts are paying off, as its José Luis Piedra label has been well received. Remedios was also the region of the first Spanish *vegueros* (planters) in the seventeenth century.

- **Oriente**. Oriente is a historical region in the island's eastern province. Legend has it that here, and more precisely at Baracoa where they landed, Christopher Columbus and his crew first discovered the joys of tobacco. Today these vast plains are almost exclusively cultivated for cigarette production.

CIGAR COUNTRY - Vuelta Abajo -

The best tobacco in the world grows in the elevated, reddish,f soil.of Vuelta Abajo. Comprised of seven sectors divided into some fifty *vegas,* or plantation sections, these 79,035 acres (32,000 hectares) amount to only about 2 percent of the island's surface. Still, almost all Havana cigars derive from this region. (Havana cigars constitute 40 percent of Cuban tobacco production. The rest goes into the fabrication of cigars of less distinguished quality, as well as cigarettes and cigarillos.)

Best of Vuelta Abajo
Bolívar
Cohiba
Cuaba
Diplomáticos
El Rey del Mundo
Hoyo de Monterrey
H. Upmann
Juan Lopez
La Gloria Cubana
Montecristo
Partagás
Por Larrañaga
Punch
Quai d'Orsay
Rafael González
Ramón Allones
Romeo y Julieta
Saint Luis Rey
Sancho Panza
San Cristóbal de La Habana
Trinidad
Vegas Robaina

Facing page: The harmony of deep green tobacco leaves against the pure blue Vuelta sky, as fleecy white clouds drift in slowly from the sea.

Vuelta Abajo Revealed

Surprisingly, the exceptional tobacco growing qualities of this area were only discovered rather late in the game, in 1772, although the Spanish had established themselves on the island in the sixteenth century. In the aftermath of a violently quelled revolt, some *vegueros* moved west to what came to be called Pinar del Rio, where they discovered the land's exceptional soil and cultivation qualities. Meanwhile, unknown to the Spanish authorities, pirates had been well aware of these perfect conditions for decades, but were biding their time to capitalize on it.

The Perfect Alchemy of All Conditions

Vuelta Abajo is famous for having a set of environmental conditions that are unique in the world. Despite all determined efforts, the combination of soil, sunlight, humidity, and sea breezes, cannot be reproduced elsewhere. Tobacco growers have unsuccessfully tried in Jamaica, Haiti, and the Dominican Republic. In addition to the specific know-how and techniques provided by local *vegueros*, *torcedores*, and other *tabaqueros*, the tobacco that grows in each *vega* presents its own particular characteristics. San Juan y Martinez (*vega* 12) and San Luis (*vega* 13) are considered the best. With the mineral-rich, sandy soil unmatched anywhere, and the cultivation (no chemicals permitted) and irrigation techniques carefully monitored by agronomic engineers, the majority of individual *fincas* (farms) in the area produce a large variety of tobaccos: the backbone of the blends needed for making specific brands and models. The main plant types are the *criollo*, traditionally used for filler; *corojo*, considered the best wrappers; and *habana 92* and *habana 2000*, which are, respectively, hybrids of the first and second, created after the attacks of *moho azúl* (blue mildew) of 1980.

This region produces the best filler, as well as the most beautiful, flsawless, and silky wrapper leaves used in making Havana cigars.

There is no doubt that Vuelta Abajo is a land blessed by the gods.

CIGAR COUNTRY - The Dominican Republic -

The Dominican Republic is situated on the eastern part of the Caribbean island of Hispaniola (Haiti is located on the west). The Dominican Republic has a long tobacco history. Like the Taino in nearby Cuba, the indigenous people on this island also cultivated and smoked tobacco. And in both places, Columbus' crew were the first European witnesses of the practice.

A Little Help From History
For a long time tobacco growing was a more or less underdeveloped enterprise here. Seeds from Cuba had been imported at the beginning of the twentieth century, so when the Cuban Revolution took place, and America sought new sources for their growing cigar market, the stage was set for serious tobacco cultivation to begin. With the U.S. embargo on Cuba in 1962, the coup d'état in Nicaragua in 1979, and persistent political instability in Honduras, the way was more than prepared for the Dominican Republic's ascension. Today no one would deny the high quality of its cigars.

The Other Promised Land
The similarity of the island's soil and climate to Cuba's has attracted several major cigar producers since the 1980s. Here, General Cigars (Partagás, Ramón Allones, Canaria d'Oro), Consolidated Cigar Corporation (Montecruz, H. Upmann, Don Diego), Fuente, Davidoff and others found not only promising natural and economic conditions, but also people with encouragingly entrepreneurial and innovative mindsets. The greatest Dominican cigar success stories usually concern the endeavors of particularly strong-willed individuals. Like the subtle flavors and fine cigar tastes they produce, these local industrial leaders are highly appreciated by their counterparts in the United States.

Best of the Dominican Republic
Arturo Fuente - Ashton - Bauza - Davidoff -
Don Diego - Dunhill - Juan Clemente -
La Aurora - La Flor Dominicana - Laura Chavin -
Macanudo - Montecristo - Nat Sherman -
Partagás - Pléiades - Royal Jamaica -
Santa Damiana - Vega Fina

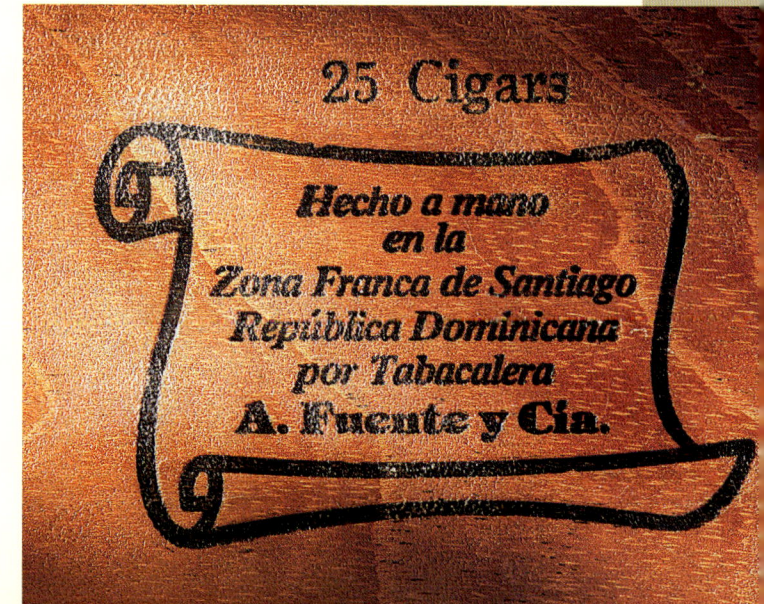

A Thriving Market

With 350 million premium cigars exported annually (two thirds of which are consumed in the United States), the Dominican Republic is now the number one producer in the world. The passion for Dominican cigars cannot be denied, and the demand has led to the creation of about a dozen brands in the last few years. But the Dominicans have been careful not to squander their reputation. During the past thirty years they have concentrated more and more on fabrication techniques, and have proven consistently creative in developing methods of cultivation, tobacco blends, and aromas.

Subtle Blends

The best plantations are located on the island's northwest side, and more specifically in the Yaque Valley, which some people compare favorably to Vuelta Abajo.

There are three primary varieties of tobacco grown in the Dominican Republic: *olor dominicano*, also known as *chago diaz*, praised for its subtle and smooth taste; *piloto cubano*, which derives from Vuelta Abajo seeds and has a rich, more powerful taste; and *san vicente*, a hybrid of the second which is lighter and more acidulous.

For the moment, since their tobacco is light in color and taste, Dominican cigar makers often look elsewhere for filler and wrapper tobacco. Stronger Honduran, Mexican, and Brazilian tobaccos are utilized for the filler, while the wrappers of the best Dominican cigars come from Connecticut, Cameroon, and Ecuador.

Thanks to their vigorous sense of innovation and market savvy, it probably won't be long before the Dominicans are growing superb wrapper tobacco themselves.

CIGAR COUNTRY - Honduras -

Neck and neck with Cuba for the position of third largest exporter of handmade cigars in the world, Honduras has built its reputation for quality cigars over the past fifty years. As in Cuba and the Dominican Republic, tobacco was smoked here before the arrival of Christopher Columbus (in 1502). And as with the Dominican Republic, before the Cuban Revolution the tobacco here was almost exclusively grown for internal consumption.

Great Beginnings
Cuban tobacco growers began resettling in Honduras in 1960. With them came much foreign capital and Cuban tobacco seeds. The Cuban seeds were crossed with local plants, and the investments grew quickly into large-scale operations. By 1962 tobacco barons such as Fernando Palacio, Dan Blumenthal, and Franck Llaneza had launched or resuscitated Belinda, Punch, and Hoyo de Monterrey on Honduran soil. In 1972 the United States Tobacco International conglomerate confided the production of its brands to Honduras.

When the political situation in Honduras—where Nicaraguan anti-Sandinista guerillas were based—stabilized in 1990, the tobacco industry really took off. The Honduran tobacco industry even managed to weather large-scale crop damage by Hurricane Mitch Òin 1999. Cigar reserves were substantial enough to cover market demand while plantations were being repaired and restored.

The Evolving Crop
There are three main growing zones in Honduras. The best tobacco comes from Jalapa Valley in the southeast. Some compare the quality at Danlí, Morocelí, and Talanga to that of Vuelta Abajo. The plantations of Santa Rosa de Copán are located in the country's western high altitudes. The Sula Valley, in the northwest, is the site where many of the fist emigrants from Cuba settled.

Several varieties of tobacco are cultivated here. Unlike the Dominicans, the Hondurans grow a good deal of tobacco from Connecticut seeds. This enables them to produce handsome, dark brown wrapper leaves. *Copaneco* is the only indigenous tobacco in cultivation. *Criollo, cojo,* and the recent hybrids *habana 92* and *habana 2000* are also grown.

Honduran cigar makers also blend Dominican, Costa Rican, and Ecuadorian tobaccos for their cigar filler.

Fine Mild Cigars
Honduran cigars are much appreciated for their smoothness and mildness, as well as for their fine quality taste and aftertaste. More than 60 million a year are imported by the United States, and they are increasingly gaining favor in Europe. The future of Honduran cigars looks bright.

And yes, proud as they are of their cigar's specific qualities and the local expertise that goes into making them, the Hondurans are still willing to accept favorable comparisons with Havana cigars.

Tobacco leaves are constantly checked as they dry.
Dangers include parasites, over drying and damp rot.
For these reasons drying huts are always well-aerated.

HECHO EN HONDURAS

Cedro Real de bosque
tropical húmedo bajo manejo

Best of Honduras
Cuba Aliados - Bances - Don Ramos -
Don Tomás - Excalibur - Flor de Copán -
Flor de Selva - Indian Tabaco Cigar

CIGAR COUNTRY - Nicaragua -

The beginnings of Nicaragua's tobacco history resemble those of some of its neighbors. It was colonized by the Spanish in the sixteenth century, and it was not until the U.S. began looking for places with favorable tobacco-growing conditions that cigar production took off and serious exportation began.

Promising and Shaky Starts
It wasn't until the 1960s that cigar aficionados began to appreciate Nicaragua's cigar-producing capabilities. The Joya de Nicaragua brand met with universal approval. When the Cuban José Padrón began production in this country in 1970, it was a boon to the local tobacco industry. But Central America was the site of many political conflicts during the seventies and eighties, and the struggles between the Sandanistas and Contras in Nicaragua was no exception. Cities, towns, and agricultural areas were ravaged, with plantations set aflame, crops pillaged, and factories destroyed. On top of this, the blue mildew blight of the 1980s attacked all tobacco indiscriminately, including reserves.
It took a good ten years after the end of the Sandanista government in 1988 for the Nicaraguan tobacco industry to attain the strong and solid reputation it currently holds. It suffered once again in 1998 when hurricane Mitch, which also hit Honduras hard, led to a mini-exile of *tabaqueros* to Costa Rica.

A Land of the Future
The serious players (from every level of prodution) are back now. For Nicaragua not only shares a border with Honduras, it also shares its neighbor's extremely fertile conditions, with similar sandy soil and high humidity levels. The main cultivated areas are the Jalapa Valley (around Estelí and Ocotal) in the northeast, and Omotepe Island, in the center of Lake Nicaragua, where Connecticut tobacco is raised for wrappers, and *criollo* is grown as binder and filler tobacco. Blue mildew resistant *habana 92* and *habana 2000* are now also cultivated.

The government plays a large role in financing and encouraging the farming of cultivatable land. This, in addition to the low cost of materials and labor, has assured the amazing quality to price ratio of Nicaraguan cigars. If you add the ancestral know-how of the labor force, and the ever-increasing quality of the product, output of fine Nicaraguan cigars can only increase.

Best of Nicaragua
Joya de Nicaragua
La Meridiana
Padrón

MORE CIGAR COUNTRIES 1
(Mexico, Costa Rica, Ecuador, Jamaica, Brazil)

Mexico

The history of tobacco consumption probably begins in Mexico. The Maya cultivated *Nicotiana tabacum*, a plant endemic to the Yucatan Peninsula, some 3,000 years ago. It was considered sacred, and was smoked only by high priests as a means of access to communication with the gods. During this period, it was also used for therapeutic and medicinal purposes, especially to treat fever. After gaining its independence in 1821, Mexico began developing its tobacco industry. The beginning of the U.S. embargo on Cuba in 1962 led to greater international distribution.

Today Mexico is the fourth largest supplier of handmade cigars to the U.S., with 10 million per year. The plantations, located in the San Andrés Valley of Veracruz, produce an excellent dark tobacco which is perfect for wrappers. The two main varieties cultivated are a local *criollo* and plants deriving from Sumatra seeds. The latter were brought over by Dutch growers who were forced to leave Indonesia after World War II. Mexican cigars are known for their balance, consistency and competitive prices.

Premier Brands: Cruz Real, Excelsior, Santa Clara, Te-Amo, and Vera Cruz.

Costa Rica

This nation whose name means "rich coast" is located to the south of Nicaragua. It became a serious cigar force in the wake of Hurricane Mitch in 1998, when the devastation of many Nicaraguan plantations led to the exile towards Costa Rica of many a cigar master. Nicaraguan wrapper leaves are rated among the best.

Premier Brands: Bahia Gold, CAO.

Ecuador

Tucked between Colombia to the north and Peru to the east and south, Ecuador's tropical climate is well-suited to tobacco growing. Connecticut tobacco grown here responds wonderfully to the climate, and the resulting wrapper leaves are highly sought after, because of their quality and their price.

Premier Brands: Ecuador does not produce its own cigars, but it provides wrappers for premier Honduran cigars (Bances, Cuba Aliados, Habana Gold), Dominican cigars (Bauza, Sosa), and Nicaraguan cigars (Joya de Nicaragua).

Jamaica

When Columbus arrived in *Xamaica* or "the land of springs" in 1494, he discovered the Arawaks smoking rolled tobacco leaves. The large-scale tobacco plantations began after 1655, with British control of the island, as did the establishment of manufacturing sites around Kingston. For a long time Jamaican cigars could only be found on the English market. While a taste for them developed in the United States after the embargo of Cuba in 1962 (to the tune of 15 million cigars per year nowadays), Jamaican cigars are still largely unknown to the rest of the world.

The tobacco plants grown here derive from Cuban as well as Dominican, Mexican, and Honduran seeds, and cigar wrapper leaves come from Connecticut, Brazil, and Indonesia.

Premier Brands: Cifuentes, Macanudo, Temple Hall.

Brazil

Brazil is the second largest exporter of tobacco leaves in the world (at just under 300,000 tons a year), with a history in the business that dates back to the sixteenth century.

There are many large plantations located in the state of Bahia, with the best tobacco coming from Mata Fina, Mata Norte, and Mata Sul.

Brazilian cigars are increasingly prized, especially by aficionados in the United States, who enjoy their full-bodied flavor.

While their dark wrappers give them a hardy appearance, they combine a fullness and smoothness in the smoking. Germans—including Konrad Adenauer and Helmut Kohl—have also been great fans of Brazilian Suerdieck cigars.

Premier Brands: Don Pepe, Suerdieck.

MORE CIGAR COUNTRIES 2
(United States, Canary Islands, Indonesia, Philippines, Cameroon)

United States

The United States is the world's number one producer as well as the number one consumer of cigars. But paradoxically, since U.S. cigars are machine-made (labor costs make handmade production impossible) they are lacking in both aroma and taste—at least when considered in relation to fine cigars made elsewhere. In general American cigars are green, often sweetened, artificially flavored, and matted (wrappers are buffed and dusted with tobacco powder).

While the American tobacco industry was born in Virginia, Florida is the number one producer today, specializing in the fabrication of cigarillos. There are also several thousand acres of tobacco fields in Maryland and Kentucky. The jewel of U.S. tobaccos is grown on Connecticut plantations, where about 2,500 acres (1,000 hectares) of sandy clay soil yield the best (and the most expensive) wrapper leaves in the world. Growers long ago turned to growing tobacco under immense gauze strips which protect them from overexposure to the sun.

Premier Brands: Hava Tampa, Grenadiers. These are industrially produced cigars; not to be confused with handmade cigars such as La Gloria Cubana, which have appeared in the last twenty or thirty years.

Canary Islands

If Canary Island cigars haven't become a major international force, it is not due to lack of experience. Cigars have been produced on these islands for quite some time. Most plantations are located on La Palma, the western-most island in the archipelago, where filler tobacco is grown in the high altitudes of Breña Alta, and the fine brown wrappers characteristic of the region are grown in Caldera del Tabariente, to the north. Canary Island growers have for a long time employed Cuban cigar manufacturing techniques, and these islands are the last place in Europe where cigars are still made by hand.

Premier Brands: S.T. Dupont, Peñamil, Vargas.

Indonesia

Land of pipes and opium, the Indonesians did not become interested in tobacco leaves until the nineteenth century—even though the plant was introduced to their shores two centuries before that. Indonesia's continued production of handmade cigars is part of the legacy of Dutch colonization.

Tobacco is grown on the islands of Sumatra, Java, and Borneo. Sumatra produces a brown tobacco whose

You may come across small cigar shops here and there in the United States, where cigars are rolled by hand. Florida and California are the best states to look for these miniature galeras, "just like in the old country." Their cigars are usually rolled by Cuban immigrants.

smooth, thin leaves make excellent wrappers. Wrapper leaves are also grown on Java, but they are not quite as respected in the cigar world. The filler tobacco known as "Dutch flavor" is grown on Borneo. It is dry, with a slightly bitter taste and an uncomplicated flavor.

Premier Brands: Calixto López, Montague.

Philippines

People in the Philippine cigar industry insist that Ferdinand Magellan himself brought tobacco to Manila in 1521. The seeds are said to have come from Brazil. The Philippines is one of he largest tobacco-producing nations in Asia. Its glory days as far as cigars are concerned date to the nineteenth century, when Havanas were the only cigars considered on a par with "Manila" cigars—and not the other way around! Today they are not as greatly appreciated because they are strong, bitter, and low in taste.

Premier Brands: Double Happiness, La Flor de la Isabela.

Cameroon

Back in the 1980s the production of premium all-Cameroon cigars appeared imminent. Unfortunately they are still awaited.
Most plantations are located in the Bertoua region, near the eastern border with the Central African Republic.

Premier Brands: While Cameroon produces no cigars of its own, some of the premier Dominican brands, such as Arturo Fuente, La Aurora, and Montecruz, use Cameroon tobacco for wrappers.

TOBACCO CULTURE:
FROM SEED TO THE CASA DE TABACO

Tobacco methods vary somewhat from country to country, but the essentials remain constant. Cuban tobacco culture serves as the paradigm. For hibernal tobacco, *vegueros* begin preparing the earth at the end of August. The growing season extends from October to the end of March or the beginning of April. The seven-month system runs as follows. Wrapper plants are transplanted to the fields first, followed progressively by filler plants through the month of November. Those planted at the beginning of November are harvested at the end of January, those from mid-November, at the beginning of March, those from the end of November at the beginning of April. The soil is left to renew itself during the intervening months. Plants are 3 to 5 inches (8 to 13 cm) when they are transplanted from the *semillero* (nursery), and have grown to nearly six feet (1.75 m) three months later.

Amazing Beauty
Every moment of the tobacco growing process presents a breathtaking contrast between red earth and the plants' striking green leaves. But when the giant cotton gauze sheets (*tapados*) are spread above the wrapper plant fields (*caballerías*) to protect them from excess rain and parching winds, the view is truly spectacular. These "porous greenhouses" are erected as the plants grow, to assure optimal conditions for their development. Because these leaves are destined to be the outer covering of cigars they must be absolutely perfect. They are cultivated to be large, homogeneous, and utterly spotless. Rather than contributing to the maturation of flavorful tobacco, the gigantic, diaphanous white scrolls spread out over the fields serve to ensure that the leaves have an impeccable appearance.

Careful Picking of Leaves, "Tier by Tier"
Plants cultivated for binder and filler are known as *tabaco del sol*. Like *tabaco tapado* (tobacco grown for wrappers), *tabaco del sol* is grown in six "tiers." Counting from the bottom up, they are called *libre de pie, uno y medio, centro ligero, centro fino, centro gordo,* and *corona*. The leaves are also picked from the bottom up, one level every week. In this way an overall quantitative accounting of how many leaves there will be per *cosecha* (harvest) is known.

Leaves also gain in intensity as they grow, and the *cosecha* of each level takes place at approximately one week intervals. Careful harvesting of each tier at the proper time is an important preliminary to blending tobaccos when cigars are rolled.

Drying and First Fermentation
Full leaves, including their stalks, are harvested by hand and then carefully transported to *casas de tabaco* (tobacco huts). These are the small, well-ventilated wooden structures where tobacco is dried. Leaves are tied together in twos (sometimes called "hands") and hung from wooden rods. After a period of one to three months, they will have lost most of their moisture. Their color changes from green to yellow to light brown as they reach maturity, attaining optimal flavor concentration. The leaves are then ready to be gathered into *gavillas* (bundles) for the crucial stage of first fermentation. This takes between three and eight weeks, depending on whether the leaves are to be used as wrappers, binder, or filler. They are then ready for the more serious second fermentation stage after the *escogida* selection.

Left: Tapados *protecting wrapper leaves from sun and wind.*

Right: Hanging tobacco leaves in a casa de tabaco, *where drying and the first fermentation take place.*

FABRICATION: THE TORCEDOR'S ART

Before the *torcedor*'s hands touch any tobacco it must go through the following stages. As it evolves into to its final color, all bitterness disappears and its complexity of flavors develop.

The Second and Third Fermentations[1]
After drying in tobacco huts, expert buyers from the *fábricas* make their way to the *escogida*, the "selection house" where leaves are sorted and ranked. The wrapper leaves are re-humidified and grouped into *tercios* (sheaves). They are then wrapped within *palmas reales* (palm leaves), which allow for both better fermentation and air flow.

Filler tobacco is treated in barrels at high temperatures and shifted frequently for aeration. Progress is checked several times a day, and the process takes a little more than a month. Next comes the second selection stage, where every leaf is checked to ensure that it is suitable for use in cigar production. Finally, the tobacco undergoes the third fermentation stage, which lasts from one to three years, depending on the quality of the batch. The highest quality tobacco is often aged longer. And so we enter the realm of the *torcedor*.

1. This traditional description of the process is misleading. The "second" and "third" fermentations are really two phases of the same process.

A Precision Art
The rollers are the royalty of the *fábrica*. The secrets of their art have traditionally been handed down from father to son and from mother to daughter. Women have for some time been the specialists in what is called stripping, the removal of tobacco leaf stems. The speed, agility, and gracefulness with which they flatten the leaves and remove the central vein is astounding. After being sorted by size and color the leaves go under the *torcedores*' knives. Mini machete-like blades called *chavetas* are used to remove remaining veins from the leaves before rolling.

When *torcedores* roll cigars they are responsible for producing a particular model, with specifications to the minutest gram and the millimeter. All their artistry goes into making sure that the combination for each cigar is uniform, in order to assure the consistency of the burn and draw. Each *torcedor* sits with five mounds of tobacco before him or her: the wrapper, the binder, and the three kinds of filler. Of these, *ligero* is the strongest, *seco* is the most aromatic, and *volado* is the must combustible. First the *torcedor* takes up a half wrapper leaf, which he cuts at both ends. Then he takes two half leaves of binder and rolls them into the three pressed-together filler leaves (the four together are known as a *muñeca* or doll), which he then rolls into the wrapper, sealing it with a tasteless, plant-based resin. Finally, the *torcedor* fashions the rounded cigar head from wrapper trimmings, clips any protruding leaves, and cuts the foot, before gingerly smoothing the body of the cigar with the blunt side of the *chaveta*.

Man Versus Machine

For a variety of reasons, usually directly relating to labor costs, many brands have opted for mechanized production. The United States is the world's number one producer of cigars, but almost none of these is *hecho a mano*, or *totalmente hecho a mano*. They have, on the other hand, perfected what is known in the industry as the "sucking machine," which continuously "chain smokes" sample after sample for quality control. Sucking machines are also used in the Dominican Republic. There's no substitute, however, for a handmade cigar. Fine, thin wrappers can only be handled by a *torcedor;* machines would tear them in a second. Great handmade cigars depend on the dexterity, experience, and know-how of the *torcedor*.

GALERAS: TOBACCO TO CIGAR

The *galera* is the heart of the *fábrica*, the workshop where cigars are made. The term *galera* is Cuban, and derives from the early days when the labor force in cigar manufacture was primarily comprised of prisoners. The way that the workspace floor is arranged, with the *torcedores* concentrated in silence at their long rows of *vapores* (workbenches), is still evocative of ships' galleys.

A Well-Kept Secret
One of the most curious aspects of the *galeras* is that they often work to produce cigars for competing brands. Thus Bolívar, Cohiba, Ramón Allones and La Gloria Cubana are produced within the Partagás factory. Montecristo, Diplomáticos, Vega Robiana, and others are rolled in H. Upmann *galeras*. This happens because even though the roller is given extremely precise indications concerning the blend of tobaccos to be worked with, he or she is never told which cigar band will be put around it before it reaches the market. The placing of the band or cigar ring takes place far from any *galera*, under the equally precise hygrometric conditions of an *escaparate* ("closet").

Galera Names
Just as every brand has names and designations for particular formats and models, cigar makers have established another level of extremely precise classification. A "lonsdale" for instance may be designated as a dalia or a cervantes; a "gran corona" by corona gorda, corona grande or cazador. These designations are called *galeras*,[1] and are presented from largest to smallest size in the other volume of this two-book set, along with their characteristics (size, diameter, and ring gauge).[2]

> **The Galley Reader**
> The tradition of the galley reader dates back to the days when someone sat in the factory space reading to the prisoners who worked tobacco into cigars. The practice eventually evolved from being a way for the authorities to keep an eye on the prisoners to a means of entertainment and or education. These days factory workers have high standards, and readers audition for the position.

---

1. There are 52 Cuban galeras.
2. Ring gauge is the diameter of a cigar, indicated in terms of sixty-fourths of an inch increments.

The orderly alignment of vapores on the factory floor dates back to the days when Cuban cigar manufacturing was the work of prisoners. But the ambience has changed, and the torcedores' silence has to do with their dedication to their work, as well as their attention to the gallery reader's words.

Galera	Length (inches—mm)	Diameter (mm)	Ring Gauge	Model
Pirámide	6⅛ —156	20,64	52	torpedo
Campana	5½ —140	20,64	52	torpedo
Exquisito	5¾ —146	17,82	45	figurado
Gran Corona	9¼ —235	18,65	47	especial
Prominente	7⅝ —194	19,45	49	double corona
Julieta 2	7 — 178	18,65	47	churchill
Corona Gorda	5⅝ —143	18,26	46	gran corona
Robusto	4⅞ —124	19,84	50	robusto
Hermoso No. 4	5 —127	19,05	48	robusto
Dalia	6⅗ —170	17,07	43	lonsdale
Cervantes	6½ —165	16,67	42	lonsdale
Corona Grande	6⅛ —155	16,67	42	gran corona
Corona	5⅝ —142	16,67	42	corona
Mareva	5⅛ —129	16,67	42	petit corona
Almuerzo	5⅛ —130	15,87	40	petit corona
Minuto	4⅜ —110	16,67	42	très petit corona
Laguito No 1	7½ —192	15,08	38	gran panetela
Delicado	7¼ —185	14,29	36	gran panetela
Panetela Larga	6⅞ —175	11,11	28	panetela

QUALITY CONTROL

The noble excellence of the finest cigars is the result of numerous quality control inspections at every stage of production. Manufacturers are intensely aware of the fact that their cigars must meet the increasingly exigent demands and expectations of today's aficionados.

The Taste Test
Once the rollers' work is complete cigars are bound into bundles of fifty, called "half wheels," with little cards indicating the *torcedor*'s reference number and the date of fabrication. After having passed tests for size, diameter, consistency, compactness, texture, and color, they are subject to the in-house *fábrica*'s taste test. Tasters have rigorous standards for rating cigars on the five following criteria:

• **Draw:** Seven levels spanning from inordinately smooth to deficient.
• **Strength:** Eight levels running from very strong to very light.
• **Aroma, combustion, taste:** Six ratings from excellent down to poor.

A cigar's characteristics, and therefore how it will be enjoyed, are comprised of these five factors taken together. Notes on the taster's blind verdict are

Left: A guillotine cutter used by torcedores *to fashion the foot of cigars.
This is an essential stage in the production of any cigar, since every model has precise size standards.
This image, however, is not entirely true to the production process, in that cigar rings are actually affixed at a later stage.*

Below: The quality of the cut is extremely important. It influences how effectively a cigar will light, which in turn affects combustion and draw.

Under Watchful Eyes

While the *torcedor* commands great respect, his or her work is subject to strict rules. There are in fact several grades of *torcedor*. The rolling of premium cigars is confided only to the most experienced and the most skillful *torcedores*. Obviously, the best cigars are also those that are the most closely inspected. Some twenty percent of these *torcedores*' cigars are subject to more or less random testing. Usually, no more than two of a roller's cigars from a single batch are found to be slightly defective. If more than two cigars fail any of the tests then the whole batch is examined. If more than four percent are rejected the *torcedor*'s salary is docked.

carefully taken and handed over to a manager, who maintains the coded list of number to roller, and uses the information for quality control and adjustments. When a cigar receives a bad rating the manager asks the taster to justify the verdict. If one taster's verdict differs greatly from the others, that taster then smokes another cigar from the same lot. If the taster holds firm in a negative evaluation the cigar is rejected, unrolled and examined closely. Once a defect has been confirmed, the cigars from the same series by the same *torcedor* are rejected and the *torcedor* is taken to task.

Visual and Tactile Checks

Next, a specialist examines the head shape and foot definition. He or she then picks ten cigars at random from the "half-wheel" and checks their color, shape, wrapper consistency, and tightness. Overall look and suppleness are of utmost importance. The tactile tests also check rolling quality, a determinative aspect of combustion values.

In some cases the problem requires that a *torcedor* re-roll the cigar in a new wrapper. Those vitolas that are deemed unacceptable (*rezagos*, literally "laggards") are put aside to be smoked by employees.

Additional quality checks take place when cigars are sorted by color, when cigar rings are placed on them, and when they are boxed by *envasadores*, experts in arranging cigars. *Envasadores* array cigars chromatically from darkest to lightest, with the darkest cigars on the left. Such nit-picking attention to detail at every point is a guarantee of excellence.

CIGAR ARCHITECTURE

What is a cigar? Rudyard Kipling ends a famous stanza from "The Betrothed" with "but a good cigar is a smoke." Okay. But what else is it?

We have seen how tobacco is grown, the secrets of the maturation process and the complex and painstaking attention required in fabrication. We know how much patience and devotion is required at every stage of the growing and fermentation processes, and how much skill is required from picking tobacco to rolling to testing cigars. But now let's look at the details of a cigar's composition.

The Key Number, 3
A cigar is comprised of three main parts, whether you look at it lengthwise or examine it through its breadth. In the first case, it is composed of the head which you put in your mouth, the body in the middle, and the foot which is the end that you light. Some smokers describe the quality or maturation of a smoke in terms of the movement from head to foot as a cigar burns. It basically starts out drier, becomes more full and complex, and ends with a more unctuous finish.

Going from inside out a cigar is made up, first, of the filler, a blend of tobacco (in Cuba *seco, ligero,* and *volado,* referred to on page 24). The primary characteristics of the cigar's taste derive from the filler blend.

The filler is wrapped inside the next layer, the binder, which is usually comprised of two half leaves of lesser caliber than the outside leaf, or wrapper. The binder serves to hold the filler in place in such a way as to assure lighting and draw quality.

A cigar's appearance, its initial allure and the impression it makes on the eye is almost entirely based on its wrapper. But what this outer surface tells about the cigar is not merely skin deep, since it bears witness to the quality of both its manufacture and its conservation. The wrapper should be smooth, regular, and unblemished. Green spots are signs of excess chlorophyll, and mold produces gray or whitish residue. Tiny white spots are acceptable. They come from slight overexposure to humidity, and can be removed by brushing. Beware: if your cigars have holes in them they have been attacked by tobacco beetles (*Lasioderma serricorne Fabricius*).

"Totalmente," "Hecho," or "Machine"?
So far we have been paying homage to the methods and practitioners behind the making of the finest cigars. But not all cigars proceed from the same painstaking procedures. There are in fact three kinds of fabrication.

• **Totalmente a mano**. The designation "*Totalmente a mano,*" sometimes also indicated outside Cuba as "hand made" or "made by hand" is an absolute category. From the blending of filler tobacco on, all the cutting, trimming, pressing and rolling operations are performed by hand, by a *torcedor*—with the aid of his or her handy *chaveta*. The novice may be astounded by the uniformity and precision of the *torcedor*'s work, and the expert can discern minute variations from cigar to cigar—positive proof of its existence as a human art.

• **Hecho a mano**. This traditional appellation is no longer current in Cuba, where it has officially been

Right: This outstanding sampling displays the range of finely crafted cigar head shapes, whether straight, pointed, or rounded.

changed to *Hecho en Cuba*. It designates a cigar whose outer covering is hand rolled. Depending on the manufacturing company, either the binder and wrapper, or the binder alone, is executed by hand.

In this type of cigar, the filler (*tripa corta*, made of diced leaves), is worked into place with the aid of an instrument designed solely to assure high consistency—and high yields. This results in a loss of flavor which cigar aficionados deplore.

• **Machine**. The fast track. Machine-made cigars currently make up nine tenths of the market, an indication of the process's success when using mediocre tobacco.

The binder is usually made of diced tobacco, not leaves, and the coarser, less oily wrappers are machine-positioned and cut. A good *torcedor* can produce about a hundred cigars a day. Machines pour out between four hundred and eight thousand an hour. There is little point in comparisons.

LARGE MODELS

From right to left (smaller than actual size): Montecristo "A," Romeo y Julieta Exhibición N°2, Trinidad Fundadores, Partagás 155th Anniversary (Salomones, ring gauge 48, 7in. [18 cm], a very promising newcomer format), Saint Luis Rey Churchills, Rafael González Slenderellas, La Gloria Cubana Médaille d'Or N° 2, Rafael González Lonsdales, H. Upmann N° 2.

Our tour of the range of cigar models will be presented in descending size order, including mention of exceptional nonstandard formats.

Nonstandard Models
These models include distinctive formats created for the sheer pleasure of their artistic effect, as well as some models made for special occasions honoring or commemorating people or events. Their unique shapes, sizes, braids, etc. are not mass-produced, and can be counted as collector's items.

Especial (Gran Corona)
Topping 9 inches (23.5 cm) in length, with a ring gauge of 47, this is the largest classic format cigar.
See: Hoyo de Monterrey Limited Edition, and Montecristo "A" (gran coronas).

Double Corona (Prominente)
A format of mythical proportions, and the longtime favorite of true cigar connoisseurs everywhere, double coronas measure 7⅜ inches (19.4 cm), with a ring gauge of 49.
See: Hoyo de Monterrey Double Corona, Partagás Lusitanias, Punch Double Coronas, Ramón Allones Gigantes, Romeo y Julieta Exhibición N°2, Vegas Robaina Don Alejandro.

Churchill (Julieta)
Yes, these 7-inch long (47 ring gauge) cigars are named after the famous English statesman.
See: Bolívar Coronas Gigantes, El Rey del Mundo Taínos, La Gloria Cubana Taínos, H. Upmann Sir Winston, Punch Churchills, Quai d'Orsay Imperiales, Romeo y Julieta Churchills, Saint Luis Rey Churchills, San Cristobal El Morro.

Dalia
This format has taken on the name of its originating *galera*. It was formerly known as a lonsdale, or a super-lonsdale. It is 6¾ inches (17 cm) long, with a ring gauge of 43.
See: Bolívar Inmensas, Cohiba Siglo V, La Gloria Cubana Médaille d'Or N° 2, Ramón Allones 8-9-8 Varnished.

Lonsdale (Cervantes)
This 6½ inch (16.5 cm) 42 ring gauge format was designed for Lord Lonsdale. It makes for an elegant, distinguished looking cigar.
See: La Gloria Cubana Sabrosos, Partagás Lonsdales Cabinet Selection, Rafael González Lonsdales, Sancho Panza Molinos.

Figurado (Pirámide, Campana, Exquisito)
The heads of these models all come to a point, a feature which amplifies tobacco taste. Length varies from 5½ to 6⅛ inches (14 to 15.6 cm) and ring gauge runs from 45 to 52. The torpedo is the best known variety.
See: Cohiba Millennium 2000, Diplomáticos N°2, H. Upmann N°2, Montecristo N°2, Partagás Pirámides Limited Edition, San Cristóbal La Punta, Vegas Robaina Únicos (pirámides), Bolívar Belicosos Finos, Romeo y Julieta Belicosos (campanas), Cuaba Exclusivos (exquisito).

MEDIUM-SIZED MODELS

From right to left (smaller than actual size): Cohiba Coronas Especiales, Hoyo de Monterrey Le Hoyo des Dieux, Cuaba Exclusivos, H. Upmann Magnum 46, Ramón Allones Coronas Cabinet Selection, Romeo y Julieta Belicosos.

Mid-size cigars are the most in demand these days, since they are best suited to current lifestyles. The pace of contemporary life, along with the full taste and improved range of medium size models since the 1980s, has led many a serious cigar smoker away from larger models.

The comfortable size of the robusto cigar (usually about 5 to 6 inches, 12 to 14.5 cm) and its rich and complex taste has led to its great popularity in recent decades. And the petit corona is a good bet as a future favorite.

Robusto, Hermoso N°4

The robusto measures 4 9/10 inches (12.4 cm), with a ring gauge of 50, while the hermoso measures in at 5 inches with a ring gauge of 48.

These models combine relatively short smoking time with rich aromatic experience. They won favor with the new generation of cigar aficionados seeking high quality that can be enjoyed more quickly.
See: H. Upmann Connoisseur N°1, El Rey del Mundo Cabinet Selección Choix Suprême, Romeo y Julieta Exhibición N°4, Saint Luis Rey Regios (hermosos N°4). Bolívar Royal Coronas, Cohiba Robustos, Juan Lopez Selección N°2, Montecristo Robustos Limited Edition, Partágas Série D N°4, Ramón Allones Specially Selected (robustos).

Corona Grande

This is a "new family" of cigars whose name derives from the *galera*—proof of the demand for cigars of this format, and the method for coming up with their names. All three of the cigars mentioned here in this category measure a hair over 6 inches (15.5 cm) and have ring gauges of 42. They were formerly catalogued as coronas, gran coronas, and lonsdales.
See: Cohiba Siglo III, Hoyo de Monterrey Le Hoyo des Dieux, Punch Super Selection N°1.

Gran Corona (Corona Gorda)

At 5 5/8 inches (14.3 cm) with a ring gauge of 46, this format develops a fine palette of flavors. Do not confuse it with the Gran Corona *galera* whose cigars measure 9 1/4 inches (23.5 cm), with a ring gauge of 47.
See: Cohiba Siglo IV, Hoyo de Monterrey Épicure N°1, H. Upmann Magnum 46, Juan Lopez Selección N°1, Punch Royal Selection N°11, Punch Black Prince, Punch Super Selection N°2, Rafael González Coronas Extra, Saint Luis Rey Série A, San Cristóbal La Fuerza.

Corona

Until robustos took over, the corona, also approximately 5 5/8 inches (14.2 cm), but with a ring gauge of 42, led the medium-sized cigar market. This fine smoking format is still extremely popular.
See: Partagás Coronas Cabinet Selection, Ramón Allones Coronas Cabinet Selection, Romeo y Julieta Coronas, Sancho Panza Coronas.

SMALL MODELS

From right to left (smaller than actual size): Ramón Allones Petit Coronas, Gérard Père et Fils 444, H.Upmann Connoisseur N° 1, San Cristóbal de la Habana El Préncipe, Cohiba Siglo I.

In no way should small format cigars be overlooked: they too play an important role. You don't have to be a sociologist to realize that the pace of daily life often calls for smoking a petit corona rather than a churchill. But first a warning for the neophyte cigar-smoker who may wish to begin with smaller cigars: some lack all subtlety, and may even be harsh, bitter, and more pungent than you might expect. Since their smaller size necessitates greater compression of tobacco during fabrication, less oxygen can combine as they burn, making for less smooth, even troublesome, combustion. Of course those we are presenting here are among the best, and will not present such difficulties. These cigars will surprise you with their freshness, rich aromas, and spicy taste.

Petit Corona (Mareva, Almuerzo)
Both the mareva and the almuerzo are approximately 5⅛ inches (12.9 cm, with a ring gauge of 42 for the first, and 13 cm with a ring gauge of 40 for the second). Because of their excellent ratio of smoke-time to flavor, they are a favorite of many of today's cigar smokers.
See: Bolívar Petit Coronas, Cohiba Siglo II, Partagás Petit Coronas Cabinet Selection, Por Larrañaga Petit Coronas Cabinet Selection, Punch Petit Coronas, Punch Royal Selection N°12, Rafael González Petit Coronas, Ramón Allones Petit Coronas, Saint Luis Rey Petit Coronas (marevas). Hoyo de Monterrey Le Hoyo du Prince (almuerzo).

Très Petit Corona (Minuto)
At 4⅜ inches (11 cm) with a ring gauge of 42, this small model is best smoked in the morning when its freshness and energy will have the optimum effect.
See: Partagás Shorts, Ramón Allones Small Club Coronas, San Cristóbal El Príncipe.

Panetela (Laguito N°1, Delicado Panetela Larga)
The elegant formats that comprise this category are not, properly speaking, small cigars. They are usually thought of as longs, although their slender ring gauges preclude classifying them with large models.
At 7½ inches (19.2 cm) and a ring gauge of 38, the laguito N°1 leads the class, followed by the delicado at 7¼ inches (18.5 cm); ring gauge 36, and the panetela larga, at 6⅞ inches (17.5 cm); ring gauge 28.
See: Cohiba Lanceros, Trinidad Fundadores (laguitos N°1). La Gloria Cubana Médaille d'Or N°1 (delicado). La Gloria Cubana Médaille d'Or N°3, Rafael González Slenderellas (panetelas largas).

Cigarrito and Demi-tasse (Laguito N° 3, Entreacto)
We only mention these formats in passing, because they do not provide sufficient flavor or body to be of interest to us in this book.
The laguito No 3 is 4½ inches (11.5 cm.) with a ring gauge of 26, and an entreacto is 3⅞ inches (10 cm) with a ring gauge of 30.

COLORS

Wrapper tobacco accounts for between 5 percent and 7 percent of cigar taste, but its aesthetic value is tremendous. Texture, pliancy and sheen are important, but a wrapper's attractiveness resides most of all in its color. And every smoker has preferences—and even prejudices—concerning the topic.

The first widespread misunderstanding: the darker the cigar the stronger it will be. In fact a wrapper's attributes cannot overcome the makeup of the filler, the real body of the cigar, in which the blend of tobaccos accounts for its taste. Second misconception: the wrappers of the best cigars are only of certain colors. No, there are wonders in every shade. Only spots, cracks or holes are sure signs of diminished quality.

A Question of Position

A cigar's definitive color is not primarily the result of maturation. Tobacco color is primarily the result of leaf position on a growing plant. From the *libre de pie*, the lowest "story," to the *corona* or "top floor," it is the leaf's lifespan itself that counts. The higher the leaf the more exposure it has had to the sun and the more full of sap it will be. Thus, for no matter what kind of tobacco, higher leaves will be darker than those lower down, which are more shaded from the sun. In addition the topmost leaves are the last to be picked.

An Infinite Color Palette

Describing the characteristics of every cigar color tone is impossible, considering the infinite palette of leaf shades and nuances. While Cuban experts claim to rely on a scale of ninety-two colors, we'll content ourselves with this practical presentation of the main chromatic categories.

• **Clarísimo**: Green (from yellow-green to light olive). North Americans have been great fans of *clarísimo* cigars, especially in the nineteen fifties and sixties. Obtaining the color requires limiting leaf exposure to the sun, and then "fixing" it with exposure to charcoal fumes. Fortunately the leaves don't take on the taste of charcoal—but they lose their own flavor in the process. These wrapper shades are particularly lacking in aroma, and because they do not undergo the same sort of maturation process as most other wrapper leaves, they are subject to cracking and do not keep for long.

• **Claro**: Light blond (*claro claro*) to brownish yellow (*claro*), this range of tones is also known as gold. It was especially popular in the 1960s. The leaves come from the lower tiers of the tobacco plant, having been less exposed to the sun. Of this light-colored group, *claro* leaves are picked later in the season and are more mature.

• **Colorado**: Light brown (*colorado claro*) to red-brown (*colorado*), all have a nuance of fire in them and a

It's up to the escogedores, *and* escogedoras *to classify cigars according to color. The difficulty entailed can be explained by the fact that Cuban authorities count 92 official tones. When boxed, cigars are arranged, starting from the left, from darkest to lightest.*

suggestion of ocher. Coming from higher up on the plant, these leaves have basked longer in the sun, producing what to our eyes are the most attractive hues. The cigar smoking public of the last twenty years largely agrees.

• **Maduro**: Rich brown (*maduro colorado*) to very deep brown (*maduro*), leaves in these tones derive from the top of the plant and are the most frequently used wrapper choice. The extent of their exposure to the sun makes the leaves ample, developed, and oily. Their flavor is strong and intense; recommended for experienced aficionados only.

• **Oscuro** or **Negro**: Dark brown to black. Only those leaves from the top of the plant, having profited from optimum sun and developed to complete maturity, can acquire these colors. They are full-bodied, harsh, bracing, and usually come from Brazil or Nicaragua; recommended for the rare connoisseurs who can handle their intensity.

BOXES AND CABINETS

Besides the rare cigar that is distributed individually, such as José Gener's Magnum, and a few premium brands that are sold in groups of ten, cigars are sold in boxes of twenty-five or in "cabinets" containing either twenty-five or fifty. Both kinds of container are made of cedar, which has a double advantage. Cedar's natural scent so closely resembles tobacco's that it is neutralized, yet is so bitter that it puts off even the most ravenous of insects. The manner in which cigars are arranged is different in each case.

Boxes
There are three traditional box types:

• **The Traditional 25-Cigar Box**: The traditional box, sometimes called a flat-top, contains two rows of cigars, twelve on the bottom and thirteen on the top (another of its nick names is the 13-topper); some brands separate them with a sheet of cedar wood. They are always perfectly aligned, with a chromatic homogeneity that is the result of the conscientious work of the *fábrica*'s *escogedor*, whose expert eye can distinguish between the hundred-odd nuances of tobacco color. Each vitola is dressed with a cigar ring affixed at exactly the same distance from its head, and a fine sheet of waxed paper is sometimes placed on top of the row. The cigars are arranged so that minor visual anomalies, such as slightly bulging veins in a wrapper, are not faced upwards. This is done for purely aesthetic reasons, since such characteristics have no influence on a cigar's taste.

Cigar box fabrication is usually the object of considerable attention, particularly on the inside. Interior surfaces are white, and upon opening the box you will usually find a *vista* ("view"), a distinctively colorful sheet of paper printed with an image designed by the brand. (See page 42.)

• **The Natural Wood Box**: These boxes are made of unvarnished cedar and are longer and wider than the sort just described.
  Their primary advantage is in providing more space, enabling each cigar to retain its cylindrical shape. The "8-9-8" box derives its name from its three-tiered packing system.

• **The Varnished Box:** The difference between this and the natural box is the varnish.
  One last detail: there are two box-closing methods, the traditional hook-closure and the pressure button.

Cabinets

This cube-shaped receptacle is used for the best models of a particular line, and the packing system is known as cabinet selection. Cabinets may be varnished or not; in either case they have slide tops and contain a neat bundle of cigars; either a half wheel (fifty) or a quarter wheel (twenty-five). A gold colored ribbon with the brand name is cinched around the cigars, then the bundle is wrapped loosely with waxed paper, which also serves to lift the cigars out of the cabinet.
A curved cedar sheet protects them from the top. The reasoning behind the conservation of top-of-the-line cigars in this fashion is understandable enough. Cigars age well over longer periods of time in such an environment. The aging process is comparable to that of a fine wine in a magnum bottle. But most of all, being stored in this way enables cigars to maintain their perfect elegance and roundness. In the final analysis, it comes down to a matter of taste.

Comparative Advantages
Cabinets:
• Better conserve proper moisture levels. Air can circulate freely and moisture filtration is unhindered, since there is no paper "barrier" between cigars. This is especially true when the cabinet is made of natural, unvarnished wood.
• Keep cigars round.
• Allow the entire selection to be surveyed at once, by lifting the bundle by the golden ribbon.
• Offer the exhilarating experience of handling all of the cigars at once.
• Make for better aging and longer cigar life-spans.
• Provide attractive cases for beautifully shaped gems.

Boxes:
• Present undeniable advantages for storage.
• Protect cigars extremely well, especially when traveling.
• Present an irresistible picture of well-ordered beauty in its perfectly aligned and ring-bearing members.

Left: A traditional box. The white background shows off the neat alignment of cigar rings, making the cigars look more squared.

Above: The cabinet selection, with a protective cedar sheet and waxed strip, helps maintain the unringed cigars' roundness.

VISTAS, PAST AND PRESENT

  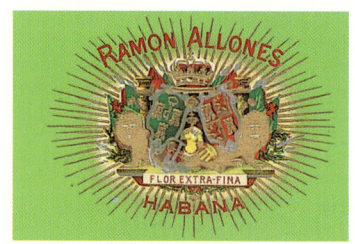 

According to legend, it all began when Ramón Allones decided to decorate the boxes of La Eminencia cigars in 1845. Since then, thousands of colorful and ornate *habilitaciónes* (literally, "outfittings") followed.

Vistas are one of the main attractions of traditional cigar boxes. With their representations of religious, bucolic, mythological, and even historical scenes, *vistas* are much more than mere ornamentation. Often taking inspiration from important moments in their brand's inception, they imbue the cigar's identity with legendary status.

The Delicate Art of Boasting

Vistas serve the double impact of offering an attractive and interesting image while signaling a brand name in such a way that it is immediately recognizable. This is why the lithographic artists who create them have customarily found ways of linking the brand to the loftiest symbols: the allegorical figure of Liberty with her flowing hair, the Virgin Mary, the horn of plenty, portraits of elected, royal, and other heads of state, and so on. Bright colors set off with gold predominate in images that not only emphasize the quality of the product—which the *vistas*' representations of numerous medals from competitions throughout the world could achieve on their own—but also endeavor to encompass and extol both the people involved in crafting the cigars, and those who smoke them. This is why a number of fictional heroes and authors have figured on these elaborate labels.

Different Times, Different Motifs

These days, *vistas* are simpler and more subdued than they used to be. They tend to represent aspects of daily life, the land, or history. Scenes of working the land, *vegueros*' faces and local landscapes are now favored subjects, probable reflections of evolving perspectives and aspirations. Even the content of dreams changes. We have presented a wide variety of *vista* styles here, but all share an undeniable wealth of inspiration, real warmth, and verve.

Above: A small selection of vistas *illustrates a range of styles, from graphic to medal-ornamented.*
Right: An assortment of vintage vistas, *all of them collectors' items.*
Above: A small selection of vistas *illustrates a range of styles, from graphic to medal-ornamented.*
Right: An assortment of vintage vistas, *all of them collectors' items.*

CIGAR RINGS, PAST AND PRESENT

Anillos (rings) are a cigar's crowning ornament. The ring, also called the band, is usually placed on a cigar after fumigation, that is just after an *escogedor* has completed the color selection before placing cigars in a box. The ring is a cigar manufacturer's seal and cachet. Anywhere in the world, under any circumstances, and at any time a cigar is to be savored, this band is what immediately distinguishes one cigar from another.

Gustave Bock's ID
Legend has it that Spanish aristocrats invented the ancestor of the cigar ring when they made a habit of tying a ribbon around their cigars to protect their gloves from staining. But the most commonly agreed upon version of the origin and spread of the ring concerns one Gustave Bock, a Dutch merchant working out of Havana in the 1850s. Bock found the means of distinguishing his cigars from others' by adapting a custom which honored a guest by printing a ring with his or her name. He established the practice for all the cigars he exported, thereby also lending his cigars an added appeal. On October 15, 1854, the Havana Union of Cigar Manufacturers officially sanctioned the practice.

Red and Gold
As soon as the practice was universally adopted, the race was on for the most elegant, rich, and strikingly identifiable band. Red and gold became the colors of choice. The amazing inventiveness of their sumptuous designs became successful marks of distinction between brands. Many models never even reached the commercial market, notably those created for special occasions, one-time events, or private functions—which of course delight collectors of these limited-edition works.

Then and Now
Modern cigar bands are often more restrained and discreet than their ancestors, and include awareness of their commercial role. What seems to count in today's world of marketing and communication are clarity, precision, and what can be ascertained with a glance. Thus a cigar ring might bear the brand name, maybe the country of origin, and that's it. Explicitness rules. But there are many devotees of the old-style marvels, which are still found on premium brands. . . and which can also be purchased at auction.

Cigar rings vary from the simple to the ornate, but all share rich coloring, usually a combination of gold, red, black and white. While recent rings often display pared-down style, collectors tend to favor older, more elaborate or Baroque motifs.

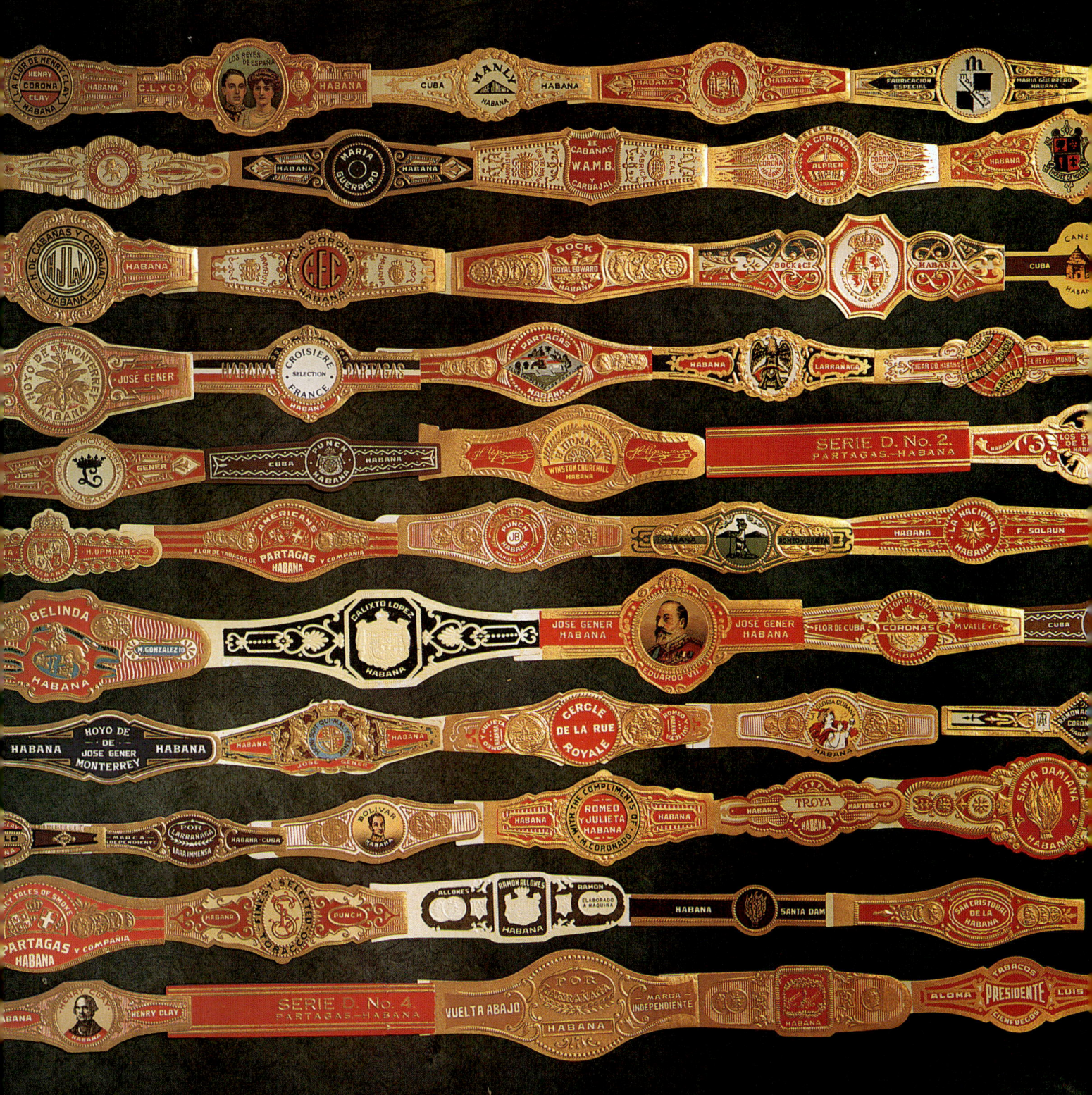

MOISTURE AND PRESERVATION

Cigar preservation is a hotly debated topic, with many points of view on methods and ideal conditions. Cigars are sensitive. They react almost immediately to any change in temperature or hygrometry. Thus it takes very little to "kill" a cigar. If dry cold is the worst enemy—causing the body to stiffen, the wrapper to tear, and the taste to become bitter and caustic—heat and excess moisture are hardly better—causing cigars to swell, mold to grow, and an excessive fermentation, which adds up to a furry effect on the palate. As in many things, a happy medium is recommended to assure full flavor expression.

The Importance of Hygrometry
Before buying a cigar it is important to be sure that it is in good condition. As obvious as this advice may seem, try not to forget it, since many cigar retailers, whilst managing to maintain diverse stocks, are not as rigorous about hygrometry as they should be. Sometimes they even present cigars inside their original tubes or cellophane. Realize that a wounded cigar cannot be healed. At best it will only continue to suffer until it dies completely.

Humidity of approximately 70 percent is the generally accepted level in which vitolas can flourish for the full extent of their lives, fifteen-odd years for the finest cigars. After that they begin to lose flavor and potency.

Consistency, First and Foremost
Most cigar lovers, even newcomers, have enough sense to realize that cigars cannot be left in the sun or in front of a south-facing window. But you should also realize, if you don't have a storage unit, that placing your cigars in the refrigerator, for instance when you leave for vacation, is just as devastating. Cold will kill a cigar quickly.

The ideal temperature range is from 63 to 68° F (17 to 20° C). But temperature itself is not the essential factor. Cigars cannot survive excessive, sudden or repeated "climatic variation." A cigar may be able to withstand a somewhat cold or hot atmosphere for a while, but "thermal shocks," especially repeated ones, are a death sentence. Good preservation conditions mean, above all, consistent conditions.

Dry English Taste
Every cigar aficionado has heard tell of the "English taste" for drier cigars, where 60 percent humidity levels are much more common.
But this "taste" is really more of an acquired habit. It dates back to the days when tobacco was imported in as dry a state as possible in order to keep import taxes based on weight at a minimum. This is why generations of English smokers have been consuming relatively dry cigars.

Left: There is no better way to test the state of a cigar's preservation than by pressing it firmly with your finger. Within a few minutes a properly humidified vitola will resume its original shape.

Above: Cigar jars have made a comeback in recent years. They make excellent humidors. (See page 49.)

THE HUMIDOR: FROM WOOD TO ALTUGLAS

If the long-term humidification that professionals are engaged in requires much knowledge and finesse, there are a number of products on the market today that make the task less difficult for the amateur. All you need do is select the humidor that best suits your kind of consumption, considering factors like cigar models, frequency of smokes, and lifestyle. The range of possibilities is great, both in terms of shape and material, as well as in the functions they offer.

The Wood Humidor
This is the oldest sort of storage system. Stylish, distinguished looking, and often intricately crafted with sophisticated woodwork, it's primary value is aesthetic, whether in an office or comprising an entire room. One problem is its variable levels of efficiency: cigars at the top will be well—and sometimes too—humidified, while those at the bottom dry out and lose all their original suppleness. In addition, if one stores a variety of models of diverse brands and formats, the mixture is liable to create a haze of combined scents that nullifies each cigar's particular aroma. That is, if the wood itself, after years of storage, doesn't impregnate your cigars with a rancid taste. True, there is a great variety of qualities in different wood oils, the way the wood is worked or pieced together, or whether or not it is varnished. We prudently advise, however, that wood humidors be used only for small quantities of cigars over short periods of time. Or even better, in taking advantage of their unquestionable elegance, that they be used mainly for presentation or display.

The Altuglas Humidor
The Altuglas is of much more recent creation. Because glass is a material that assures much more homogeneous, long-term preservation, cigars maintain their individual personalities. Preservation quality is even increased if cigars are left in their original boxes: the cedar wood takes on the double role of filter and humidity sensor.

If the tobacco is too dry it will draw upon the humidity within the wood, and if there is too much moisture, the wood will absorb the excess, thereby protecting the wrapper's integrity. The Altuglas' main virtue is retaining proper humidity levels for long periods of time. Rehumidifying is in order only about once every three months, of course according to taste, and after verifying the need by checking the hygrometer.

> **A Miracle Formula**
> To enjoy your cigars at their best, here's our advice:
> • Preserve your *puros* in their original box inside a humidor.
> • Then transfer them into a jar, where they will recover their strength and form.

There is such a large selection of humidors on the market today that every cigar lover can find the best method for his or her needs.

Left: An Altuglas humidor with integrated hygrometer.
A leather-covered traveling box; very elegant, but not effective for long-term preservation.

One necessary precaution: keep an Altuglas clear of any heat source (radiator, fireplace, sun) since the combination of humidity and heat will activate tobacco fermentation, something you definitely don't want. Finally, to assure perfect hygiene, change the water every six to eight months—never use soap— and the padding every three years or so.

Cigar Jars

The first cigar jars appeared in the twentieth century. They were made of glass and were more like old-style apothecary jars than true humidors. They were also not tremendously efficient.

To avoid fast and complete drying out, once opened it was necessary to transfer cigars to a traditional humidor. But their beauty, such as the appealing twenty-five to fifty capacity cigar jars created by H. Upmann for their Cristal models, attracted those in the know. The century ended with renewed interest in cigar jars, this time in porcelain.

Those that we developed after years of research with the Bernardaud de Limoges porcelain specialists will keep cigars fresh, at least over the short term (about six months). There will even be some improvement in vitola density, compactness and aromatic concentration, and the wrapper will be perfectly soft and smooth.

Finally, we'll point out the recent arrival on the market of wood, humidifier-equipped cabinets, some of which are as tall as 4 feet (1.2 m). Time will tell what the future holds for these.

AGEING

Like a fine wine, a fine cigar requires painstaking efforts in order to reach the perfect state of maturity. Those who present you with cigars at the height of their perfection are specialists in this domain.

Developing Personality

Paradoxically, ageing begins well before cigar storage. From the moment it is harvested, tobacco is carefully examined. The characteristics of future blends must be gauged at this stage.

Ageing should not be confused with fermentation. Fermentation is a continuous biological process in the evolving life of a cigar. Ageing concerns the blending of different tobaccos that gives a cigar its unique taste. If one were to smoke a freshly rolled cigar one would get only a suggestion of what the future blend will taste like. Harmonization into a particular personality requires time.

Perfect Maturity

Ageing to maturity not only gives a cigar the time to attain its unique taste, it also allows it to secrete excess leaf oils, leaving just the right amount of oily matter to underscore its particular, complex aromatic bouquet. Finally, it is during this period that every vitola acquires the specific combination of rigidity, flexibility, and density that make up its tactile effect.

Successful maturation requires meticulous and constant work. Boxes must be opened regularly and cigars must be brushed off ever so carefully, one by one. Brushing removes settled particles of humidity and sawdust that block the wrappers' pores. Preservation standards are draconian at this stage to avoid "climatic disasters," when shifts in moisture levels and sharp changes in temperature would be lethal.

Cigar specialists have their individual secrets, just like oenologists and tea experts. By definition a specialist is privy to special knowledge, and so we cannot go into greater detail concerning this topic here. Still, the objective is always the same: allow each item to reach full maturity. Again, compare the process to how a fine wine must be awaited patiently until the moment when it will yield the most pleasure. And we can never repeat this enough: a cigar is a living product that requires assistance to come into its own after the series of rough changes that take place during its youth. Perfection is always our goal.

Let the Buyer Beware
Cigar aficionados visiting Cuba will naturally be tempted to acquire some fine cigars from the old *torcedores* that will pop up every once and awhile along their path. In some places, they will even roll you some *puros* to your specs and on the spot. Beware of being disappointed.
—However talented the *torcedor* may be, he or she will not be rolling you a "real authentic" Coronas Gigantes de Bolívar or Partágas Luisitanias. Remember that since *torcedores* are not privy to fabrication secrets concerning the cigars they roll, they will not be able to tell you what kind of cigar will result from the very blend of tobacco in their seasoned hands.
—A freshly rolled cigar is smokeable, but after twenty-four hours it becomes extremely bitter. So taste the "new born" right away, before excess humidity (usually absorbed off after several weeks in an *escaparate*) temporarily impairs your taste buds.
—If you decide to keep and age a cigar acquired in this way, do not store it with those whose pedigree you are sure of. Having not been fumigated it will more likely than not harbor a miniscule population that will be happy to move on to the other cigars once they have finished with that one.

Left: One of the most important aspects of the ageing process is regular brushing to keep moisture from settling on cigars.
A half-wheel of our Sélection des Sélections Gérard Père et Fils at perfect maturity.

CLIPPING AND LIGHTING UP

If there's one domain in which every aficionado has definite preferences and is more than willing to proclaim them it's the "before" of smoking.
Yes, those moments before the first puff are filled with anticipation and even longing. And we will see that the art of savoring a cigar contains essential preliminary steps. But let's not get ahead of ourselves.

The Cut

When cutting off a cigar head make sure to cut straight. Also make sure not to clip off too much of the cigar, which may wastefully accelerate combustion, or too little, which may result in reducing your access to the cigar's flavor.

These pointers aside—and even though there are cutting techniques from the innovative to the antique that aficionados swear by in the darkness of their smoking rooms—there is no one inviolable law of the blade. We will therefore present the most classic methods.

• **The Guillotine**
Guillotine cutters come in single- and double-edged versions. Whether inexpensive plastic or costly mother-of-pearl and precision blade models, they are a very practical pocket-sized option. Those with tempered steel blades are particularly effective.

• **V-Shaped Clipper**
V-shaped clippers, or V-cutters, were prevalent in the 1950s and 1960s for cutting drier cigars, but are less popular today. V-notched blades can have damaging effects on the smoking of a cigar, and in addition, cannot be used on large models.

• **Scissors**
Cigar scissors are not made to be carried around, but make handsome utensils on a desk in an office or sitting room. This fact in no way detracts from how very well they do their job. Their price is also on a par with their elegance.

• **Cigar Punches**
Cigar punches are back, after a long period of unjustified neglect. The punch is a cylindrical instrument that cuts a hole by pressure. The round openings that result are smaller than those made with most cutters but are sufficient for lighting up and adequate combustion.

• **The Cortador**
The cortador is an exact replica, slightly reduced, of the *torcedor*'s length-calibrating instrument, the *guillotina*. It is a handsome precision instrument.

Lighting Up

There are many schools of thought concerning the indispensable stage of lighting a cigar. Some moisten their cigars, others warm them with a flame, and still others soak the head in alcohol (an old Spanish custom)—all before even having recourse to a cedar wood strip, a match, a lighter, or even a candle. As purists, we cannot condone using any product that will adulterate a cigar's genuine aroma.

• Ignition Accessories

Matches, particularly long-stemmed and cedar wood varieties, and lighters—butane but not gasoline—and torch lighters are recommended, once you've mastered a technique for controlling the flame. Like gasoline lighters, candles should be avoided: both will alter the taste of your cigar.

• The Process

Simplicity is a good watchword. Hold your cigar between your thumb and index finger, not in your mouth, then bring the flame to about two inches (1 cm) from the foot. Slowly turn the cigar and put it to your lips, then bring the light up to the end of the cigar again. Pause for a moment, then draw in the first puff, which will at the same time cause the cigar to begin to burn evenly. Now you are off and running smoothly.

Take Pity on your Cigars

Some people insist upon clipping their cigars with their teeth or nails. Those unseasoned in these methods should probably avoid them. It takes a miracle or a veteran Cuban cigar-maker to get an even cut in one of these two ways without damaging the wrapper or having the smoking experience spoiled by getting stray tobacco in your mouth. At least equally devastating results can ensue to your cigar and your fingers from using a kitchen knife, household scissors, or a razor.

THE ART OF SAVORING A CIGAR

Because savoring a cigar is first and foremost a matter of enjoyment, there are no hard and fast exclusionary rules. There's nothing worse than having to listen to someone who finds it necessary to take on a tone of pompous certainty to assert the best (and only!) way to enjoy a cigar. Still, there are ways of increasing pleasure with concentrated refinements. Just as a child begins to read by making out individual letters, a smoker's palate and nose can be initiated without much difficulty to particular aromas and flavors so as to be able to discern them with greater specificity. Since you will better appreciate that which you know, here are some pointers for setting out on the road of smoker's happiness.

Five Cigar Senses
Savoring a cigar makes use of all the senses, or almost all. Hearing is of secondary importance compared to seeing, touching, smelling, or tasting, which are all vectors of the amazing sensations that an excellent vitola will arouse.

• **Looks**
Everything has led up to this moment. You take the cigar out and look it over, noting its impeccable wrapper, its sheen, its unruffled surface, its color nuances, its neatly cut ends, its round head: your eye takes it all in.

• **Touch**
Appreciate the density, the pliancy, the wrapper's texture. Slight bulges indicate imperfect rolling or the late rehumidification that will kill a cigar.
A soft roundness with no crackling and the capacity to quickly resume its original shape after having been pressed by your finger are signs of quality. In short, touch reveals the nature and intensity of the smoking experience to come.

• **Smell**
Smell your cigar before lighting it.
Its spicy, grassy and earthy qualities will already be evident. This is what Cubans call *fumar a crudo*, or "raw smoking."
   Although the bouquet changes after lighting—with some aromatic nuances dropping back and others coming to the fore—you'll already have an idea of how the cigar will evolve.

Discriminating taste involves all the senses but is, above all, the result of a refined balance between aesthetics and taste. A fine curl of smoke (left), an elegant receptacle and ashtray, like the amber of a well chosen rum, all contribute to the moment's perfection.

Terms of Discrimination

It is often difficult to describe sensations. Once again, if you take the time to distinguish and name particular taste experiences, you can then easily describe your enjoyment without sounding like a puffed up expert. Pleasure is only increased when accompanied with the right words to describe it. Here is a sampling of terms for each of the categories given above.

• *Feel*: Delicate, sensitive, soft, tender; supple, thick, soft, silky, oily, flat, dry; compact, heavy, tight, sticky, rough.

• *Nose*: Weak, short(-lived), green; verdant, subtle, fruity, oily, wood(s)y, floral, underbrush, smooth, appealing, round, cacao, young leather, tanned leather, ample, animal, amber; rough, spicy, piquant, sharp, persistent.

• *Taste*: Flat, dull, grassy, blunt; sweet, fruity, oily, wood(s)y, sugary, peppery, spicy, strong, exotic, heady, intoxicating, ripe, heavy, sharp; tangy, piquant, tannic, hot, burning.

• *Sensation*: Discreet, distant, nonexistent, monotonous; unpronounced, understated, fresh, promising, comforting, full, generous, well-rounded, broad, nourishing, muscular; oversweet, furry, persistent, gruff, hard-hitting, intoxicating, oppressive.

In all events, realize that precise language accompanies and develops with experience.

• *Taste*

Your taste buds jump to attention with the first puffs. As the cigar burns regularly you discern its aromatic depth, identify its flavors and appreciate their qualities, whether mellow, powerful, or a myriad of gratifying combinations of the two.

• *Enjoyment*

In our view, this is the real fifth sense of cigar smoking, when you relish the harmonious correspondence between the cigar's qualities and the environment, the moment, the atmosphere. You savor the vitola's richness and complexity, its balance and lasting effects.
And, suddenly, you understand the real value of those wispy clouds of smoke that rise in the air.

BODY AND FLAVOR

There are expressions which appear again and again when talking about cigars. But it isn't always easy to ascertain precisely what they mean. Here is an overview of these short explanations of some frequently repeated, and sometimes counter-intuititve, terms.

Flavor
• **Acidy:** This is a characteristic often found in young tobacco which has larger amounts of chlorophyll and starch. Its attributes sometimes diminish over time—and sometimes don't!

• **Wood(s)y:** This aroma may suggest green, dry, or wet wood. In any case it is omnipresent, with infinite, sometimes quite subtle nuances.

• **Cacao:** Usually coming out near the foot of the cigar, cacao cadences are relatively oily, rich, and heavy, and last long in your nose. They are prevalent and lingering; full and satisfying, and are accompanied by agreeably spicy notes.

• **Leather:** Different leather terms apply typically to the wrapper: young, tanned, old. High quality leathery taste is lush and persistent.

• **Short-Lived:** A bouquet that seems to disappear just after being sensed by the nose, short-lived aromas usually lack spicy accents, and present a milder range of sweeter, woodsy, and dry effects.

• **Dud**
A cigar with no beast in its belly. It makes no impact. Such ineffectual cigars are generally the product of a year with poor quality tobacco yields.
They will not improve with age. And even if they are covered with a fine looking wrapper, their effect is sadly stillborn.

• **Green**
A "green" cigar is neither fresh and invigorating, nor does it necessarily indicate a cigar's color. It is the bitter taste of young tobacco: sharp and lacking in fullness and roundness.
Do not confuse this with the green aroma given off

from older, well-stored cigars. These recoup a full range of aromas with a few minutes' worth of oxygen.

• **Earthy**
These actually include all sorts of outdoor values, suggestions of the farm, wheat, mountains, stables, and fields: a mixture of the energetic and the subtle that can be extraordinary.

Taste Types
• **Heady**
Rich, full-bodied, and abundant, but not necessarily strong levels of intensity. Especially the first half of your smoke will be oily and round with mellow tannins. Unfortunately, a heady cigar will grow hot if it has taken on too much humidity. If it is rolled too tightly it will become stifling and, smoked quickly, will burn your palate.

• **Mild:** A mild cigar may not necessarily lack taste complexity. It can have a full expanse of flavors, without extreme or overly spicy accents. The smoker remains in complete control of its pleasing consistencies, which explains the ever growing rise in the popularity of this kind of cigar.

Very often, mild cigars will leave you with a salty taste on the outside of your lower lip.

• **Spicy:** This term includes every aroma on the spice rack, from sweet to piquant, including cedar, vanilla, coffee, chocolate, cinnamon, licorice, gingerbread, pepper, and cumin. These characteristics are in fact the "spice of life" of a cigar lover's experience, and are highly sought after.

• **Dull:** Dull or boring cigars are extremely light. Whatever tastes they do have, lack intensity. They remain flat and dry in your mouth, even when perfectly humidified.

• **Unctuous/Oily:** Cigars rich in oleoresins are non-acidic and linger nicely in the smoker's mouth. This is a characteristic of the finest vintages, and the elegant patina of excellent aging. These cigars begin strong and become smother and rounder, with mellowed spicy accents, and an overall rich Madera tonality.

WHEN THE TIME IS RIGHT

Like everything that requires good taste to be appreciated, enjoying a cigar is a matter of personal taste. One cigar lover may prefer mild or light cigars, another may enjoy intensity and depth, while a third's tastes may evolve over time or differ according to circumstances. This last is probably the closest to the way it should be, in that fine cigars offer an infinite array of tastes and sensations, which vary even for the same person in relation to surroundings, mood and occasion. We are not the same every day, and neither are cigars.

That Special Moment
The last quarter century was a period when personal habits changed significantly. Cigars became products for people with Epicurean characters, those who relish quality. Whether alone or in company, this generation takes pleasure in, and knows how to appreciate, fine cuisine and excellent wine. Better yet is their delectation in preparing experiences of harmonious conviviality. Mixing the pleasures of dining with those of the cigar, or combining smoking with a long moment of solitary contemplation, are simple yet satisfyingly personal and unique experiences. Since spontaneity is never the worse for knowledge, these two or three remarks should come in handy.

Two Kinds of Cigar
Cigars can be divided into two main categories: (A) Cigars to be Savored, and (B) Friendly Cigars. We suggest considering them in terms of the time of day.

Like any great taste sensation, the taste of a cigar will vary according to your digestive state; what you have recently tasted, whether your stomach is empty or full, whether you are active or resting. To best appreciate your vitola, you must choose it with care to suit the moment.

• Morning:
(A) Rich and oily: Palates are most receptive in the morning, ready to fully experience a full range of aromatic subtleties.
(B) Fresh and mild, with spicy accents to lightly bolster the taste, but not too strong.

• After a Light Lunch
(A) A cigar with body, with a woodsy or earthy character and full presence in the mouth.
(B) Round and pleasant without requiring work, it exudes ease and freshness, like gazpacho on a summer evening.

• After a Substantial Lunch
(A) A cigar that will help your digestion, accompanied with your after-meal drink of choice. An oily, highly spiced cigar with slowish, regular combustion.
(B) No apt representative for this context.

• Late Afternoon
(A) Rich in oleoresins and preferably hard-hitting. All your attention should be focused on the cigar: no reading, writing, or other distractions.
(B) Mild to the point of being unobtrusive, with an easy burn and draw. You're taking a break, it's a reward for what you've accomplished.

• Evening
(A) Intense, powerful to the point of excess—not necessarily in terms of its size, but more importantly in terms of the depth and intensity of tastes, and the complexity and concentration of thick woodsy aromas. It's like chewing delicious gingerbread: the consistency and flavor are perfect.
(B) Strong without overdoing it, this is the cigar to smoke after a hard day at work or an evening beside the fireplace. A thinker's or dreamer's companion, it's the perfect partner to a game of chess—and you're the unrivaled master.

ACCESSORIES

The universe of cigar smoking gives rise to the creation of a great variety of genteel and elegant apparatuses and tools. These certainly have their use value, while offering interesting aesthetic echoes of all aspects of the product which inspires them. The range of accessories available today is quite extensive, running from the simplest to the most elaborate. On the following pages we present a representative sampling of what's available.

There are a great variety of cases and holders, corresponding to just about every conceivable cigar size. They are intended for transporting a few cigars without damaging the wrappers. Whether of gold or silver, leather, lizard, or crocodile skin, or some other precious material, a holder must be rigid enough to protect your vitolas, while not being so tight as to cause them to tear. At one time silver cigar cases were all the rage, carried around like a miniature flask. Today leather predominates.

Some handsome accessories by S.T. Dupont: a lacquer and silver single cigar case with matching guillotine cutter, lighter, and ashtray.
The two cigar rests on the ashtray keep cigar feet from getting damaged.

Sampling of brown and black leather cases for one, two, or three cigars.

An assortment of cigar cutters. (See also page 52). From left to right, V-cutters, round and square single blade guillotines, and folding scissors with tempered steel blades—all silver and gold plated and with tempered steel blades. To the right, varieties with red, green and black lacquer.

Rediscovered in the 1990s, punches (see also page 52) are used to create an opening in the closed end of a cigar. The opening is small, but just enough for a good smoke. Some models have more than one lance with different diameters.

CIGARS AND GASTRONOMY

It wasn't that long ago that the idea of smoking a cigar during dinner would have been considered a sin. Weren't cigar lovers banished to the smoking room the moment dessert was finished, so that the slightest wisp of smoke would not disturb the others' nostrils?
Times have changed.

In losing its superior airs the cigar has gained in substance: aficionados have more developed tastes, and above all know how to enjoy more than one kind of pleasurable experience at a time. Who would dispute that the right wine enhances the taste of a meal? Or that a superbly prepared dish will bring out the delights of a fine wine? Our palates are capable of luxuriating in other alliances as well.

Chefs to the Rescue

It is largely thanks to excellent chefs themselves that cigars have been officially and fully accepted as members of the gastronomic world. The likes of Alain Senderens, Guy Savoy, Alain Dutournier and Pierre Troisgros, among other masters, first sang the praises of Havanas and then of other vitolas as well.

To the surprise of their clients, they began offering cigars in their restaurants, where they set up comfortable smoking rooms for complete enjoyment—and where they often step in for doses of cigar talk. They will tell you about incomparable combinations, such as Bordeaux shad and Ramón Allones 8-9-8s, or their Béarnaise goose along with a Rafael González Lonsdales. Who would disagree? But note that when you consume such wonders it is best to curb your intake of sweets: they can interfere with these refined taste sensations.

Continental Cuisine

While the three pillars of continental gastronomy, French, Italian, and Spanish cuisines have as many similarities as differences among them, they share a number of cooking methods and spices. This is why, taking their resemblances rather than their contrasts into account, the same kinds of cigars can apply to all three cuisines. Similar reasoning is behind opting, for example, for an elegant Pomerol (L'Évangile, La Fleur-Petrus, L'Église-Clinet) a round and full Saint-Émilion (Magdelaine) or a voluptuous Gevrey-Chambertin (Les Combottes du Domaine Leroy).

• **Best Choices:** Very aromatic cigars, whether woodsy, earthy, or floral, that are at the same time round and rich in oleoresins. *Punch, Partagás.*

Asian Cuisine

The nature of Asian spices along with the delicate

*Menu cover for the annual luncheon of the Club des Parlementaires Amateurs de Havanes in Geneva.
These events are famous for the combination of excellent dishes with cigars—sometimes including some novel innovations—as the afternoon leads to a cigar-smoking crescendo.*

tastes of some dishes, require tremendous skill in the selection of cigars. It is especially important to aim high, since the difficulty resides in creating a subtle break between tastes that will refresh, rather than coat your palate. This may come as a surprise to some, but the perfect combination can be achieved with the inclusion of a white Loire Valley wine (Sancerre du Domaine des Ouches, Pouilly-Fumé Cuvée Silex de Didier Dagueneau) or Alsace (Gewurztraminer Epfig du Domaine Ostertag, Riesling Altenberg de Marcel Deiss).

• **Best Choices:** Mild and fresh cigars with more spicy dishes. Round, oily and woodsy cigars in company with more subtle dishes. Powerful and full-bodied cigars go well with ginger. *Hoyo de Monterrey, El Rey del Mundo, Saint Luis Rey.*

Middle Eastern Cuisine

This well-rounded, expansive, and refined cuisine goes perfectly well with strong, full-bodied cigars, as well as more subtle ones. The rich variety of flavors in each dish just asks for a cigar to be lit up between courses.

At the same time, enjoy a Riesling (Domaine Weinbach, Schlossberg Cuvée Sainte Catherine) or a Tokay-Pinot Gris (Domaine Zind-Humbrecht, Clos, Jebsal, or Rangen de Thann).

• **Best Choices:** Very aromatic, complex cigars, with earthy accents and consistent combustion, lasting in the mouth; not tiring on the palate. *Bolívar, Ramón Allones, San Cristóbal de La Habana.*

CIGARS AND ALCOHOL

As we've noted many times, alcohol and cigars are a traditional combination. Still we should go over the topic again, a bit more carefully. After all, just because some marriages are conjugal bliss doesn't mean that others aren't stormy. Since all things are subject to the influence of their company, circumstances and moods, the connoisseur will progressively discover ideal couplings, for every occasion.

Too Much of a Good Thing?
For a strong cigar, a strong drink? Nothing could be less true. Unless you are looking for a headache. The two will only clash, never meld, while anesthetizing your taste buds like over-the-counter cough medicine. This is not Epicurean. In other words, beware of excesses of enthusiasm, even with an aperitif, and treat your taste buds as if you really want to enjoy your vitola.

• **Champagne:** If it is brut or extra-brut, and you make sure not to serve it overly chilled, champagne and cigars make a delicious pair. The unexpected combination of coolness and heat will win you over. The best choice is a manageable format with aromatic, light flavor that will awaken your taste buds without overwhelming them. *Gérard Père et Fils 444, El Rey del Mundo Cabinet Selección Choix Suprême.*

• **Whisky:** Scotch, whisky, rye, and bourbon all do quite well in the company of a cigar. The peaty taste of a single malt scotch will raise a Havana cigar to new heights, while an aged whisky responds wonderfully to the elegant lightness of a Dominican. *Santa Damiana Torpedo, Rafael González Coronas Extra.*

• **Port:** Great vintage ports are a sublime complement to Havanas. Their grassy undertones and rich flavor underline the vitola's woody earthiness, while the mellifluous roundness of each contributes to and echoes the other. *Ramón Allones Petit Coronas, Juan López Selección N°1.*

• **Brandy:** Calvados, pear, plum, and other brandies have been the cigar's long term partners; cigars mix very well with these fruit flavors. Armagnac and cognac are also good choices, especially when they are smooth, full and mellow, and do not overwhelm the vitola. An overly bitter brandy can also ruin the alliance. *Hoyo de Monterrey Double Coronas, Cohiba Siglo IV.*

• **Rum:** If you've never experienced the duo of rum plus a fine Cuban cigar, you don't know the meaning of a perfect union. Common history and origin certainly make for harmony here.
We suggest that you try paring a Havana with a vintage Martinique rum; both will do their ancestors proud. *El Rey del Mundo Taínos, Partagás Pirámides Limited Edition.*

• **Sweet Wines**
Rivesaltes and Beaumes-de-Venise muscats, banyuls and maurys suit cigars quite well, especially once they have reached a ripe age and their special orange accents come out in their golden *rancio*.
These go best with a well rounded vitola capable of flattering their complexity. *Saint Luis Rey Regios, H. Upmann Connoisseur N°1.*

A Master of Hedonism
This will come as a surprise to no one. The religion of the great American writer, and eternal Epicurean, Ernest Hemingway, was taste. Early in life, Hemingway understood that pleasure is matter of precision. So, not only did he habitually choose his Cuban rum in relation to the cigar he was smoking—or was it the cigar in relation to the rum?—but, better yet, he selected his coffee in relation to the rum he was about to drink, which he had decided upon in terms of the cigar he was about to smoke—unless it was the other way around!

CIGAR SPECULATION

The recent rise in the cigar's popularity and the inroads its aromatic universe has made among new palates has led to a new market for rare, forgotten, and extraordinary specimens which appear from time to time on the auction block. These usually luxurious auctions are organized by the finest auction houses (Christie's, Sotheby's), and as with works of art, they provide passionate connoisseurs with the opportunity to acquire boxes, lots, and even single pieces.

Havana Cigars, Kings of the Market
Yes, all honor goes to the king, and until now only Havanas have aroused enough interest to warrant auction house sales. There are two main reasons for this: the extreme richness of Cuban cigars, and the disappearance or discontinuation of certain brands and models.

Pre-revolution cigars are without a doubt the champions at attracting collectors' attention. It should be mentioned that given their age, these cigars are unlikely to be excellent smokes, and are appreciated mainly as curiosities or unique pieces. In this category we can cite Calixto López, Maria Guerrero, and Henry Clay, among others.

On the other hand, post-revolution cigars are very much in demand by cigar lovers like you and me. They have been preserved under optimal conditions, and with the exception of some of the earliest vintages, they are still and can continue to be exceptional smokes. Everyone who loves vintage cigars is thus invited to bid

---

Going…Going…Gone!
On December 12, 1994, in a luxurious hotel in Zurich, Sotheby's presented one hundred lots of exceptional cigars which we had selected. In less than fifteen minutes many pieces had been sold by proxy bids from Paris, New York, Hong Kong and elsewhere.
Irked beyond words by the speed with which items were being picked up, literally, from under his nose, one determined bidder decided not to lower his hand until the auction was over. This worked out well enough for him, since he then made many fine acquisitions — but at such a rate that the bidding board ceased to function way before the end of the session!

Right: Back cover of a Sotheby's auction catalogue, illustrated by the painter Anton Molnar.

Below: Catalogue page presenting lots of Partagás Série D N°4.

Partagas D4

Type: Robusto
Diameter: 2cm
Size: 12.5cm
Colour: 'maduro' to 'colorado'
Bouquet: generous with aromas of pure cocoa
Taste: rich, powerful and instantaneous
Format: round, banded
Production: hand made in Cuba
Maturation: in the cellars of Gérard Père et Fils, Geneva

800 1 jar of 25 cigars
801 1 jar of 25 cigars
802 1 jar of 25 cigars
803 1 jar of 25 cigars
804 1 jar of 25 cigars
805 1 jar of 25 cigars
806 1 jar of 25 cigars
807 1 jar of 25 cigars
808 1 jar of 25 cigars
809 1 jar of 25 cigars

per lot: £550-700

on these rareties, which sometimes reach astronomical prices. Some notable examples: La Flor de Cano, Davidoff, Dunhill, and Romeo y Julieta Fabulosos.

"Los Especiales"
Besides those glorious representatives from the past, cigars created for unique occasions such as the anniversary of a great brand, a special event, a diplomatic encounter, or a coronation also fetch high prices. Limited series vitolas made available only to those attending a particular event obviously also have all the makings for future returns.

Cigars fabricated for the Burgundy harvest of 1988 under the patronage of the Cheveliers du Tastevin celebrated the first "marriage of the houses of Burgundy and Havana." This is an example of the production of a series of items for a special event whose value should rise over time.

Or take the Cohiba torpedos presented for the first time at the "dinner of the century," in honor of the 500th anniversary of the arrival of Christopher Columbus in America. (See page 75.)

Do the prices quoted for these articles have any real relationship to consumer interest? It is hard to say. Such occurrences are really just micro-phenomena on a global scene. Auction purchases seem to be expressions of individual passion rather than investments in items for future gains. Still, when love stories begin one doesn't know whether they will be short-lived or lifelong affairs; auction sales resemble them as the manifestation of passion, of attachment, and of the devotion to a memory.

COUNTERFEITS FROM CUBA

Like all exceptional quality and expensive products, cigars are counterfeited. Havana cigars are the most affected, including boxes, packaging, and certification labels. The only thing that can't be faked is the taste of the cigar. And since it is no easy matter to taste a cigar before purchasing, a few tips can help.

Four Golden Rules
These simple precautions will help you avoid being had.
• Only buy cigars from well-established sellers. They are vested by law with responsibility for authenticity.
• Never buy cigars over the Web, unless you are certain of the merchant's reputation.
• Avoid "one time sales" at prices that "beat out all competition." There is no good reason for a Cohiba to be pushed at a third of its value.
• Also beware of individuals who seek to sell you a portion of their stock. They too have no good reason to discount quality cigars.

Some Caveats
Besides running the risk of prosecution for being in possession of stolen goods, you may be in for some other surprises.
• The pretty boxes that you've bought, and particularly the varnished ones, are made of inferior quality wood. Rather than functioning like cedar in terms of hygrometry, they will transfer their own odors to the cigars.

• The filler of your handsome vitolas will not be made of tobacco alone, but will include the likes of banana leaves, fabric covered with any old *tripa corta*, or another substance, whose nature we will not go into more specifically here, except to say that it bears no relation to traditional blends.
• Tobacco beetles (lasioderma) may be arranging a surprise party for you. They will munch on your cigars, lay their eggs, and the newborn larvae will dig thousands of tiny holes in non-fumigated tobacco. A disaster.

Detecting Phonies
Fake box and fake cigars; real box and fake cigars; fake box, fake cigars, and fake guarantee seal; real box, fake cigars, and fake guarantee seal. This is what you need to look for:
• A box of Havana cigars must bear a government guarantee seal which, because of its green ink, is ironically called a "dollar." After a law established on July 16, 1912 this *sello de garantía nacional de procedencia* is affixed to the left corner of a box (or the right corner for cabinets of 50). The inscription is translated into English on the top of the band, into French at the bottom left, and into German at the bottom right. Make sure that it says Republica de Cuba and not some other province, such as Vuelta Abajo. You will also find the "Habanos" sticker on the right-hand corner (or the left-hand corner for cabinets of 50).

It is white with gold borders, with "Habanos" printed in red with yellow shadowing. Boxes imported to Europe may also include the stamp of the importer's code and a smoker's warning.

• The box bottoms are engraved or burnt with the inscriptions, *Habanos s.a.* (*Cubatabaco*, on old boxes), *Hecho en Cuba*, and when applicable, *Totalmente a mano*. Factory and date codes are also stamped on the bottom.

• Check inside the box, even in a restaurant, and make sure that the cigar rings form a perfectly aligned row across the cigars.

There may also be a band of waxed paper between the two rows of cigars. If so, the dimensions of this sheet should be exactly the same as that of the box, and there should be a small tab at the paper's upper right-hand corner.

Two different Sancho Panza Belicosos. At first sight the one on the left may seem more attractive (greater length, nice blond color), but it is, in fact, a rather blatant counterfeit. Not only are the dimensions and the color off, but the mediocre cut of the foot and the band are also evident, not to mention the way that the brand name is on the front of the original box and on the side of the fake.

GREAT CUBAN CIGARS, PAST AND PRESENT

An exhaustive history of Cuban cigars is yet to be told. Their stories often involve complex heroic narratives, including miraculously coming back to life and sometimes vanishing from the scene. They are of great importance to smokers who often identify with their favorite vitola, remaining faithful to it above and beyond all others. What follows is a brief excursion into the world of some of the cigar greats. Each one of them is represented in the second volume of this set, where you can read about top-of-the-line models in greater detail.

Bolívar

Bolívar takes its name from the *libertador*, Simón Bolívar, who led the Cuban revolt against Spanish power at the beginning of the nineteenth century. The brand has wondrously rejuvenated in recent years, having maintained, at least in its handmade models, its richness and strength while at the same time gaining in roundness and suppleness.
• **The Best:** *Belicosos Finos* (campana), *Coronas Gigantes* (julieta), *Royal Coronas* (robusto), *Inmensas* (dalia), *Petit Coronas* (mareva).

Cohiba

Cohiba owes the mythical status of its name as much to the exciting circumstances surrounding its creation in the 1960s as to its quality. Over the years Cohiba has further deepened its aromatic range of fruity, full-bodied and sustained tastes. A fine example of this evolution is the Siglo series.
• **The Best:** *Millennium 2000* (pirámide), *Siglo IV* (corona gorda), *Robustos* (robusto) *Siglo V* (dalia), *Siglo III* (corona grande), *Siglo II* (mareva), *Lanceros* (laguito N°1).

Cuaba

A recent brand (1996), Cuaba has adopted the unique strategy of limiting itself to a singular format, the figurado, which is considered traditional; even primordial.
The four vitolas they manufacture comprise a small range of light, aromatic and very approachable cigars. All are excellent introductions to this model.
• **The Best:** *Exclusivos* (exquisito).

Diplomáticos

These cigars entered the European market in the 1960s, aspiring to resemble the Montecristo line (N°1 to N°5 of the same format) at a lower price. Diplomáticos cigars have an enjoyable strongness that ages well.
• **The Best:** *N°2* (pirámide).

La Gloria Cubana

This old-time brand was created in 1885. It experienced all sorts of vicissitudes before solidifying its current

reputation in the 1970s. Today it offers a wide variety of cigars. La Gloria Cubana has managed to maintain its large format line at a time when others have concentrated their efforts on mid-size models.
Fans of La Gloria Cubana vitolas relish their generous and pronounced fruity aromas, as well as their rich smoothness and finesse.
• **The Best:** *Taínos* (julieta), *Médaille d'Or N°2* (dalia), *Sabrosos* (cervantes), *Médaille d'Or N°1* (delicado), *Médaille d'Or N°3* (panetela larga).

Hoyo de Monterrey

Hoyo de Monterrey cigars were born in 1865, created by José Gener, who was also the owner of La Escepción. Hoyos are characteristically smooth, light and very flavorful, with a combination of sweet and floral accents. These cigars are distinctively subtle and elegant.
• **The Best:** *Particulares Limited Edition* (gran corona), *Double Coronas* (prominente), *Épicure N° 1* (corona gorda), *Le Hoyo des Dieux* (corona grande), *Le Hoyo du Prince* (almuerzo).

H. Upmann

H. Upmann was founded in 1844 by the brothers August and Hermann Hupmann. They split the "H" from the "upmann" to have it stand for *hermanos,* or brothers, in their label. Full-bodied, earthy, and strong, H.Upmann cigars are coveted by aficionados of "old Havana" style taste. While subtlety is not their forte, they are not lacking in complexity and distinction—particularly in the cigars at the top of their line.
• **The Best:** *N°2* (pirámide), *Sir Winston* (julieta), *Magnum 46* (corona gorda), *Connoisseur N°1* (hermoso N°4).

Juan López

Its real name is Flor de Juan López, and this very old and unpretentious brand specializes in medium-sized and smaller cigars, all very finely crafted by hand. Appreciation for Juan López' light, smooth, and very flavorful cigars has been consistently high since connoisseurs in the 1980s began paying them attention.
• **The Best:** *Selección N°1* (corona gorda), *Selección N°2* (robusto).

Montecristo

Montecristo was founded in 1935 by the Menéndez and García families. It continues to be considered the archetypal Havana cigar, although recent production increases have led to periodic decreases in quality consistency.

The large models' full smoothness maintain the brand's traditional and outstanding standards.

• **The Best:** N°2 (pirámide), "A" (gran corona), Robustos Limited Edition (robusto).

Partagás

Partagás, or La Flor de Tabacos de Partagás y Cía, was created in 1827 by the Catalonian Don Jaime Partagás. It is an extremely prestigious brand. From the start, the Partagás line has proven capable of adapting to the most subtle smokers' changing palates. The signature tones are tannic, sometimes rustic, sometimes tough. Intensity, authenticity, and richness of flavor remain the most crucial aspects of the superior models from this great cigar name.

• **The Best:** Pirámides Limited Edition (pirámide), Lusitanias (prominente), Série D N°4 (robusto), Lonsdales Cabinet Selection (cervantes), Coronas Cabinet Selection (corona), Petit Coronas Cabinet Selection (mareva), Shorts (minuto).

Por Larrañaga

This brand was born in 1834 and remains a more or less well kept secret. There are about a dozen models in the line, with consistently smooth and full, honeyed taste.

• **The Best:** Petit Coronas Cabinet Selection (mareva).

Punch

This brand dates back to 1840. It has a variety of models whose woodsy and fruity taste registers develop in strength. Its conscientious fabrication procedures yield cigars of exemplary consistency.

• **The Best:** Double Coronas (prominente), Churchills (julieta), Royal Selection N°1 (corona grande), Super Selection N°1 (corona grande), Petit Coronas (mareva), Royal Selection N°12 (mareva).

Quai d'Orsay

The Quai d'Orsay brand appeared in 1974. It was launched, with a controlling interest by a French tobacco company, directly onto the French market. Orsay cigars are entirely and authentically Cuban. They are mild, with subtly accented woodsy, fruity, sometimes grassy and lightly earthy tones. They offer very good quality for their price.

• **The Best:** Imperiales (julieta).

Rafael González

This venerable brand, whose full name is Flor de Rafael González, offers some of the finest and most distinguished cigars in the world. Their rich flavors develop gingerbread overtones, their wrappers are exquisite, their effect is noble through and through.
• **The Best:** *Coronas Extra* (corona gorda), *Lonsdales* (cervantes), *Petit Coronas* (mareva), *Slenderellas* (panetela larga).

Ramón Allones

Another venerable brand (1845) for connoisseurs. Powerful and heady, these cigars belong to the Havana tradition of exacting standards and rich, earthy taste.
• **The Best:** *Gigantes* (prominente), *Specially Selected* (robusto), *8-9-8 Cabinet Selection Varnished* (dalia), *Coronas Cabinet Selection* (corona), *Petit Coronas* (mareva), *Small Club Coronas* (minuto).

El Rey del Mundo

El Rey del Mundo was born in 1882, spent a long spell in limbo, and was revived at the end of the 1980s. El Rey cigars are smooth, spry, and tend to have floral and spicy accents—in other words they are very easy smokes.
• **The Best:** *Taínos* (julieta), *Cabinet Seleccion Choix Suprême* (hermoso N°4).

Romeo y Julieta

Romeo y Julieta is one of the must illustrious brands of Cuban cigar. Its inception was in 1875, and its line of cigars is as rich in variety as it is in taste. A powerful, almost rugged flavor characterizes them all.
• **The Best:** *Belicosos* (campana), *Exhibición N°2* (prominente), *Churchills* (julieta), *Exhibición N°4* (hermoso N°4), *Coronas* (corona).

Saint Luis Rey

Relatively ignored until the 1980s this is a brand for the informed connoisseur. Saint Luis Rey flavor is earthy, spicy, lightly sweet, and above all very rich in aroma and taste. An occasional cigar smoker trying one for the first time will be in for a big surprise—and may thereafter become a full-fledged devotee.
• **The Best:** *Churchills* (julieta), *Série A* (corona gorda), *Regios* (hermoso N°4), *Petit Coronas* (mareva).

Sancho Panza

Sancho Panza began making high quality cigars in 1848. These vitolas are sophisticated and elegant. Solid and flavorful at once, they offer up unctuous, floral, sweet tastes.
• **The Best:** *Molinos* (cervantes), *Coronas* (corona).

San Cristóbal de La Habana

A newcomer on the Havana scene (1999), San Cristóbal de La Habana is already known for subtlety and smoothness, rather than intensity. It has won over the new generation of cigar smoker seeking less imposingly heavy vitolas.
• **The Best:** *La Punta* (pirámide), *El Morro* (julieta), *La Fuerza* (corona gorda), *El Príncipe* (minuto).

Trinidad

The Trinidad brand, a half brother of the Cohiba, was launched in 1998, and currently makes one kind of cigar. It has a smooth, toasty, spicy, cocoa flavor.
Try the *Fundadores* (laguito N°1).

Vegas Robaina

The name of this new brand (1997) takes its inspiration from an old Cuban plantation family. Their five vitolas are mild and very aromatic.
• **The Best:** *Únicos* (pirámide), *Don Alejandro* (prominente).

The last few years have seen the arrival of a surprising number of new Cuban brands. At least four of them are available on the international market: Cuaba (1996), Vegas Robaina (1997), Trinidad (1998), and San Cristóbal de La Habana (1999).

VINTAGE AND LEGENDARY CIGARS

Like all of the most excellent products that are aged, a cigar's life span can be long and noble. Given proper care, a cigar will reach glorious maturity. All it needs to attain legendary status is to become extremely scarce.

Into Vintage

Cigars are deemed "aged" after a period of between two and five years. After this period they come to be considered "vintage." For cigars to be "vintaged," as in the ageing of wine, they must be kept in the most suitable hygrometric and temperature environment. And, like wines, some tobaccos age better than others under these conditions. The trick is to take into account the raw materials comprising each brand, and to adapt the ageing process accordingly. Of course time itself is one of the most important factors, and the best vintages are those that have matured for a very long time. A vitola develops a wonderful roundness with age. But most of all, ageing enables the release of flavors that could not be tasted without it.

The smell of a long-aged cigar is deceptive: before lighting it will usually be very vegetal. The smoking experience itself always begins smoothly, a little flat, slightly woodsy, and even, almost, too mild. Then, tanned leather aromas and Madera accents emerge as the burn reaches the barrel. These precious tonalities bloom in the last third: oh so subtly, oily and rich.

The Effect of the 1990s Craze

Until fairly recently, England was the only country that cultivated the art of ageing vintage cigars, albeit with a different goal. For historical reasons already discussed (see page 47), the English traditionally tend to appreciate drier cigars, so the ageing process does not aim for the same results.

Interest in vintage cigars developed elsewhere in the 1980s, when aficionados began seeking rounder, more ample smoking experiences. But it was not until the next decade that the great Cuban post-revolution cigars reached stages of delicious maturity. That is when the excitement over aged Dunhills, Davidoffs, La Flor de

Left-hand page: 25 Henry Clay Diamantinos in their original glass tubes.
Left: Cabinetta, Varadero, and Havana Club by Dunhill. Davidoff 80 Aniversario, Partagás Cristal Tubos, Rafael González Vitolas B, Romeo y Julieta Romeos, La Flor de Cano Diademas.

Cano cigars, Montecristo Bs, or a vintage glass cigar jar of H. Upmanns really took off. Today, at more than forty years of age, many of them are no longer smokeable, but they are considered fine collectibles.

Legendary Cigars

Unlike vintage cigars, there is little to gain and much to lose in smoking a collectible cigar. On the other hand, they are of historical and personal interest. The prime examples are brands no longer produced (such as Henry Clay, Maria Guerrero, Cabañas y Carbajal, Joaquín Cuesta, La Corona, Villar y Villar), and vitolas no longer available (Gispert Petit Coronas de Luxe, Longos de La Escepción, Palmas Reales Cristal Tubos de Partagás).

As the last vestiges of an epoch, these pieces are sought after for their formats, their finesse, the originality of their modes of presentation, and for interest in the blends from which they were made, sometimes comprised of elements no longer available. It can also be their very uniqueness that draws people's fascination. Interest favors cigars manufactured for special occasions, anniversaries, public or private celebrations, or other unique events. Specific examples include jars of Cohiba Millennium (torpedos); luxury boxes of 1996 Partagás (50 salomones); Partagás 150th anniversary models (150 pieces in three models: 50 old-style lusitanias, 50 8-9-8s, and 50 robustos); and Cohiba's thirtieth anniversary (50 double coronas, with a special band). Along with discontinued and retired models, cigars like these—whose effects are at least as great as the sum of their parts, considering the dose of extravagancy added to their original excellence—are sure to be the legends of tomorrow.

COLLECTORS AND COLLECTIONS

There are two kinds of collecting. The first encompasses both rare cigars which are too old to smoke, and ageing cigars in preparation to be smoked. The second concerns shifting from the first category to the second, depending upon what is up for auction and the state of the market.

What People Collect

Any cigar collection entails the acquisition of quality cigars. Even aficionados of a single format (boxed double coronas for example) will not take the risk of buying everything that exists in this model—there is no sense in purchasing lousy vitolas that will age poorly. In addition to people who collect particular models, there are people who collect particular brands, and others who collect cigars from particular *galeras*. Other specialties include discontinued or forgotten models, special issues, one-of-a-kinds, *figurados*, pre-revolutioary Cuban cigars, post-revolutionary Cuban cigars, and those that are more than fifty years old. There are even people who relish collecting counterfeits! But this last is a passion of a different kind, a peripheral interest at best, since no matter how talented the counterfeiter may have been, genuine quality is surely missing.

Optimal Storage

Time, patience, and conservation means are required for a collection to grow in value. Even the oldest cigars, whose days of being smoked are long past, must be kept at consistent temperatures and humidity levels. Otherwise, they will dissolve into dust. The older the vitola, the greater the importance of climatic maintenance.

That is why we created Private Stock in 2001 (pictured opposite). Collectors can come to us to preserve their cigars in optimal conditions, under the watchful eye of a team of specialists devoted entirely to their perfect upkeep. Hundreds of veritable "safety deposit boxes" have been set up to house cigars for long-term ageing. A complex system insures round the clock regulation of conditions for every cigar, and information regarding them can be constantly checked by the individual client over the Internet. Inquiries and transactions are facilitated by Private Stock's continually posted and updated information concerning date of purchase, price, adjusted value, market reevaluation, and so on. All collectors need do is sit back and enjoy, while their cigars comfortably relax and age.

GÉRARD PÈRE ET FILS' SPECIAL BLEND

We've said it before: cigar lovers' tastes evolve. This fact has been one of our principal concerns over the last twenty-odd years. It is why we created a line of smooth and oily cigars that smoke both round and cool. Rather than redoing what was already there, our aim was to compensate for what was lacking in the gamut of available cigars by coming up with gratifying new aromas and flavors.

In other words, our objective has been to master difference and to create distinction.

The Underlying Method For A Satisfying Smoke
In the making of products that call upon the palate and taste buds, the quality of raw materials is essential for success. Cigars are no exception to this rule. For this reason we have sought out the finest tobacco plantations in various parts of central America, and closely monitor the impeccable manufacture which takes place in the Dominican Republic.

Our cigars are designed in the way that a great chef creates a dish, by harmonizing ingredients and their flavors, and responsively giving our customers what they want. Our line tends towards the mild and the subtle, like a balcony opening out onto the intensity of Cuban cigars. Our first ambition is to awaken the palate to all a cigar has to offer: a range of delicate flavors in a fine round smoke.

Refinement and Originality
We opted for large diameter cigars because they produce full, well-rounded taste, they are neither too hot nor overbearing. Our objective is that the smoker get a pure impression of the refinement of our private blend's character and originality.

• ***222:*** This is a very small, fresh corona. It is smooth, almost bland, as it points the way to things with greater intensity: a suffused flavor that comes together to awaken and charm your taste buds.

• ***444:*** A typical robusto with an excellent size to flavor ratio, the 444 will never get hot. It has a light range of flavors, whose woodsy and honeyed accents last through the final third of the cigar.

• ***555:*** A smallish torpedo, perfect for today's world. It lights easily and burns well. The floral accents and shape make for an agreeable and smooth smoke.

• ***666:*** The 666 is a gran corona with a double corona ring gauge. It becomes progressively rounder and silkier as you smoke it, with almost sweet nuances towards the end.

• ***888:*** This is a double corona *par excellence*, with the added attraction of being easy to digest. Elegant and smooth, it won't weigh you down; quite the contrary, it is exceptionally light.

All these cigars are well-rounded while you smoke them, but do not have a lingering finish. From the largest to the smallest, they are moderate cigars that will not make you work. The smaller models have distinctive personality and strong impact in the mouth. However, they will never overwhelm your palate. We plan to run a new series of cigars with oilier and rounder body, and heftier flavors. This limited blend will be another response to the call of the world's extensive cigar tastes.

LATEST TRENDS

The world of cigars is in a state of excitement. Not since the 1930s, when a multitude of large and small brands were being produced in Cuba, has the world market seen such a profusion of brands. In conjunction with the new generation's tendency to pursue novel taste experiences, this inevitably leads to innovative trends.

Taste
The gamut of taste possibilities has enlarged as a result of new modes of consumption, as well as the evolution of smokers' palates. Today's tastes tend toward the smoother, lighter, and less filling, which in no way has hindered the recent success of certain Cuban cigars comprised of strong, rich and full-bodied tobaccos. As examples of the latter, we'll mention Partagás' Pirámides and Montecristo's Robustos Limited Edition.

Models
After the rise of the churchill and the double corona, the 1980s glorified the robusto, followed by the torpedo, which eventually gained the edge of popularity. The petit corona is the cigar for this young millennium. People like it not only for its taste but also for its format and short smoking time. A petit corona takes about half an hour to smoke. In the era of the race against time, this is a feature that counts.

Personal Taste
Cigar smokers have changed, and with them, the spirit of smoking itself. No longer the unique domain of Epicurean lovers of fine wine, gourmet meals, and large vitolas, cigars are now enjoyed in less conventional settings. Lifestyles have become more inclusive, and the cigar's place has expanded, most notably in relation to women smokers. Much has also been gained in the realms of nuance and subtlety. Cigars are not only after-dinner items. They have found their way to the afternoon, accompanying people at work, and in their musings and daydreams, as well as their quiet evenings alone. People now smoke a cigar for what it specifically has to offer, choosing according to the time of day, circumstances, company, and mood. A direct link to gastronomy and to oenology has been established. The way is open for the future.

Today's Favorites
• ***Bolívar Belicosos Finos:*** After having been overlooked for a long time this richly flavorful torpedo has come to center stage, taking its place among the greatest.
• ***H. Upmann Magnum 46:*** Let's wager that this long neglected yet magnificent corona gorda will be one of the next great success stories. Its size, like its more flavorful than powerful character are perfect for current tastes.

- **Ramón Allones Small Club Coronas:** Rich and well rounded as it releases a winning range of aromas, this very short corona is a child of the times.
- **Hoyo de Monterrey Épicure N°4:** Both aromatic and smooth, this robusto offers a satisfyingly full-bodied smoke.
- **Montecristo Robustos:** The Cuban master's surprise offering that triggered renewed interest in old style Havanas with modern formats. The future is in its hands.
- **S.T. Dupont Robustos:** Very finely made on the Canary Islands, its smoothness corresponds perfectly to today's demand.
- **Gérard Père et Fils 555:** This torpedo, with its silky mellow taste, was created for today's smoker. It satisfies the need for an easy-going cigar.
- **Vega Fina Robustos:** A favorite format from a light and velvety line, this Dominican vitola is cool and slightly dry. Gentle on the ambient atmosphere, it has everything to recommend it.
- **Partagás Série D N°2:** After a long period in limbo, this celebrated robusto is back, winning people over to old-time complexity and silky taste.
- **Partagás Pirámides Limited Edition:** Another fine Cuban counter-attack, this newcomer's intensity and rich, authentic *maduro* flavor has already made it a classic.

THE CIGAR SMOKER'S PANTHEON

Whether you are a veteran connoisseur or a newcomer, one thing is certain: you're traveling in good company. The number of eminent and famous people that have smoked and sung praises to Havana cigars—and now cigars from other producers as well—is tremendous. Franz Lizst's passion for cigars is well known. Even when he was hard up, he made sure he had a few vitolas on his person. When he entered a monastery, Lizst appealed to the religious authorities so zealously that he was granted special dispensation to continue smoking. Preeminent people have been campaigning for the cigar for as long as there have been cigars.

Famous Parting Shots
During the Napoleonic era, MarshAl Michel Ney, Prince of Moskowa was shot by a firing squad at his own command. His final request before bellowing, "Soldiers, straight to the heart!" was for a last cigar. That was in 1815. It was Napoleon's troops who brought cigar smoking to the rest of Europe after they discovered it in Spain. The world of artists and literature, always ready for novelty, quickly adopted the habit. And from that day to this the number of artist, writer, musician and scientist cigar smokers is beyond counting, from Balzac to Byron, Sigmund Freud to Fran Lebowitz, from Samuel Johnson to Maurice Ravel, from Pablo Picasso to Albert Einstein. In fact, Edmund Spenser was already lauding tobacco in the *Fairie Queen* in 1590, while serious quips like these from Mark Twain, "Eating and sleeping are the only activities that should be allowed to interrupt a man's enjoyment of a cigar," and "If smoking cigars is not permitted in heaven, I won't go," have become the stuff of popular legend.

Smoking but Equal
The French novelist Aurore Dupin, better known as George Sand, was among the first women for whom public cigar smoking was a sign of independence and disdain of societal prejudices. More violent opponents of social norms, Bonnie Parker and the renowned markswoman Annie Oakley were also great aficionados. Writers like Colette, who advised that a woman take up smoking the specific vitolas of her lover to get a better handle on him, and actresses like Lillian Russell, were also great cigar smokers in their day. Lillian Russell apparently smoked 500 extra-short cigars per month, making her the female counterpart to Winston Churchill's legendary fifteen a day. Between the lips of such stars

as Demi Moore, Kim Basinger, and Whoopi Goldberg, cigars have become both a common sight and continue to add a certain flair—as they may do for men as well. Still, when Madonna lit up a cigar on the David Letterman show it caused a stir.

The Popularized Image
Today, thanks in large part to movies, which contributed to shaking off the cigar's stuffy image, the media's diffusion of images of entertainers and politicians with their cigars, as well as haute cuisine, which has given it both cachet and a green light, cigars are no longer the prerogative of certain classes of society. They belong to the Epicurean in every walk of life.

Hollywood has certainly had its cigar smoking icons. Classic examples of stars who, intentionally or not, altered the image of cigar smoking, at least in the characters they played, are Edward G. Robinson, Charles Laughton, Robert Mitchum, Jerry Lewis, Dean Martin, W.C. Fields, and Orson Welles, as well as George Burns and Groucho Marx. Today a great number of actors, film-makers, and people in all sorts of media, sports, and creative fields calmly and unostentatiously smoke cigars. Consider Michael Jordan, Luciano Pavarotti, Peter Falk, Bo Derek, Francis Ford Coppola, Jeff Goldblum, Cindy Crawford, Antonio Banderas, Sharon Stone, Wayne Gretzky, Vanessa Williams, Tom Hanks, Dany De Vito, Puffy Combs—the list goes on and on, not to mention politicians, such as Rudolph Giuliani and Bill Clinton, or the great international chefs cited earlier.

All Things to All People
If the most famous cigar smoker is still probably Winston Churchill, who consumed some 250,000 double coronas in his lifetime, these days it is impossible to describe a single person, or kind of person, as the incarnation of "the cigar smoker." Whether the experience takes place alone or is shared with another, it is, more than ever, not an obsession or a flighty infatuation, but rather a deep-rooted taste that connotes no extravagance, hype, or ostentation. Like the uncorking of a fine bottle, a cigar can be enjoyed with friends or can accompany calm and solitary meditation.

Women have always smoked cigars. The days when George Sand startled society are far behind us, and the number of women connoisseurs is still on the rise. Left: the author with his sister Marie-Christine, an important and expert participant in the running of Gérard Père et Fils.

CIGARS DU JOUR - Level 1 (Novice) -

Here is an ideal selection of cigars for the novice cigar smoker. Of course it is only a suggested list, but it is based on experience garnered over many years of talking with and advising smokers.

Morning
Gérard Père et Fils 222. This very short corona won't cloud your palate. It is fresh-flavored and smokes quickly.

After a Light Lunch without Alcohol
Gérard Père et Fils 555. Flavorful and mild, round and oily, easy to smoke—these are the hallmark qualities of this satisfying torpedo.

After a Light Lunch with Alcohol
Cuaba Exclusivos. The fresh, woodsy exquisito (figurado) gradually develops oilier and spicier inflections without overtaxing the smoker's palate.

After a Substantial Lunch with Alcohol
El Rey del Mundo Cabinet Selección Choix Suprême. Fresh and easy, this "smoker-friendly" hermoso N°4 (robusto) is mellow and flavorful, with an amazing lightness.

Afternoon
S.T. Dupont Robustos. Elegant and unimposing, the ease with which this cigar smokes is astounding. It burns perfectly and is never boring.

Apéritif
Give your palate a break to get ready for dinner.

After a Light Dinner without Alcohol
Rafael González Petit Coronas. Vegetal with woodsy notes, the difficult finish on this mellow and flavorful mareva is a fine suggestion of things to come.

After a Light Dinner with Alcohol
La Gloria Cubana Médaille d'Or N°1. A quality, extremely elegant, delicado (gran panetela) with distinctively easy combustion for this format.

After a Substantial Dinner with Alcohol
Quai d'Orsay Imperiales. This woodsy, flavorful and mellow julieta (churchill) is perfect for introducing the novice to a model that is usually heavier and less accessible.

From top to bottom and left to right: Rafael González Petit Coronas, Cuaba Exclusivos. Gérard Père et Fils 222, Quai d'Orsay Imperiales. El Rey del Mundo Cabinet Selección Choix Suprême, Gérard Père et Fils 555, La Gloria Cubana Médaille d'Or N°1, S.T. Dupont Robustos.

CIGARS DU JOUR - Level 2 (Amateur) -

This selection is aimed for the cigar smoker who is already acquainted with different cigar formats and is familiar with a reasonably broad range of flavors.

Morning
San Cristóbal de La Habana El Príncipe. This cool and vegetal minuto (petit corona) gets the day off to a fine start.

After a Light Lunch without Alcohol
Padrón 1964 Anniversary Coronas. Rich and flavorful, this dry cigar will not linger too long in your mouth after smoking.

After a Light Lunch with Alcohol
Arturo Fuente Perfexción Opus X Robustos. A fine, oily and flavorful Dominican cigar with no spicy tones. Perfect for topping a light meal.

After a Substantial Lunch with Alcohol
Rafael González Coronas Extra. This corona gorda (gran corona) will win you over with its floral aroma, easy combustion, and wonderful balance.

Afternoon
Gérard Père et Fils 444. A very agreeable robusto. The freshness and generous combustion will unpretentiously satisfy your palate until evening.

Apéritif
La Gloria Cubana Médaille d'Or N°3. Light in its first third, then intensifying, this woodsy and rich panetala larga is probably the easiest smoke of its kind.

After a Light Dinner without Alcohol
Por Larrañaga Petit Coronas Cabinet Selection. This aromatic cigar develops fine floral notes which make it very appealing. Its roundness and ample finish should provide a high level of satisfaction for the amateur.

After a Light Dinner with Alcohol
H. Upmann Connoisseur N°1. This unassertive, accessible hermoso N°4 (robusto) is well-rounded but not heavy, and smokes quickly and quite pleasingly.

After a Substantial Dinner with Alcohol
El Rey del Mundo Taínos. A julieta (churchill) that is cool, light and accessible while remaining interesting from beginning to end. An excellent introduction to large models.

From top to bottom and left to right: Rafael González Coronas Extra, Por Larrañaga Petit Coronas Cabinet Selection, El Rey del Mundo Taínos, La Gloria Cubana Médaille d'Or N°3, Arturo Fuente Perfexción Opus X Robustos, Gérard Père et Fils 444, H. Upmann Connoisseur N°1, Padrón 1964 Anniversary Coronas, San Cristóbal de La Habana El Príncipe.

CIGARS DU JOUR - Level 3 (Aficionado) -

At this point we enter the world of vitolas with a deeper range and diversity of tastes. These are cigars that reward the smoker's pleasurable engagement. This selection is designed for the experienced smoker with a developed palate.

After Breakfast
Partagás Shorts. This minuto (petit corona) is a real wakeup call. It is fresh and full of flavor, casting vanilla and flowery accents to perfectly spark your day.

Morning
Cohiba Siglo III. A large, subtle, and mild corona for starting the day with polish and finesse.

After a Light Lunch without Alcohol
Partagás Coronas Cabinet Selection. Noble and ample, this high tradition Havana gets straight to the point, filling the palate with its very rich flavors.

After a Light Lunch with Alcohol
San Cristóbal de La Habana La Punta. A pirámide (torpedo) that never lets up. The evolution of taste as you smoke is amazing, especially considering its youth.

After a Substantial Lunch with Alcohol
La Gloria Cubana Médaille d'Or N°2. Rich and intense, this is a real thoroughbred dalia (churchill). Its spicy and woodsy notes are the crowning touch to a fine meal.

Afternoon
Saint Luis Rey Regios. This smooth and lightly woodsy hermoso N°4 (robusto) is very approachable; a fine afternoon companion.

Apéritif
Ramón Allones Small Club Coronas. More than a sure bet for a minuto (petit corona), this excellent, round, flavorful cigar prepares your palate for the evening.

After A Light Dinner without Alcohol
Hoyo de Monterrey Le Hoyo des Dieux. Fruity and oily rich, this high quality cornona burns slow and smokes easy, delivering a superb flavor medley.

After a Light Dinner with Alcohol
Romeo y Julieta Belicosos. The perfect polish to a dinner—of seafood, for example—this heady aromatic campana (torpedo) is an intense experience.

After a Substantial Dinner with Alcohol
Partagás Lusitanias. This powerful, tannic, and intense prominente (double corona) is one of the best there is.

From top to bottom and left to right: Saint Luis Rey Regios, Hoyo de Monterrey Le Hoyo des Dieux, San Cristóbal de La Habana La Punta, Romeo y Julieta Belicosos, Partagás Shorts, Cohiba Siglo III, Ramón Allones Small Club Coronas, Partagás Coronas Cabinet Selection, La Gloria Cubana Médaille d'Or N°2.

CIGARS DU JOUR - Level 4 (Connoisseur) -

This is a selection designed with a consummate connoisseur in mind, one with strong tastes who typically smokes strong, full-bodied cigars throughout the day.

After Breakfast
Punch Super Selection N°2. As it fills your mouth with its range of earthy and spicy flavor, the bracing effect of this excellent corona gorda will set you off on your day with a blast.

Morning
H. Upmann Magnum 46. With its excellent size to ring gauge ratio, this more flavorful than powerful corona gorda is an amazingly easy smoke.

After a Light Lunch without Alcohol
Juan López Selección N°2. Smooth, light, and cool but not intense, this corona gorda is less concentrated than other cigars of its format—which is why it will hit the spot after a light lunch.

After a Light Lunch with Alcohol
Partagás Série D N°4. Very flavorful and heady, this is a robusto with tons of personality. For connoisseurs with strong tastes, this cigar will pack your palate.

After a Substantial Lunch with Alcohol
H. Upmann Sir Winston. The strength of this julieta (churchill) makes it especially appealing to those whose palates are excited by heavy amber and woodsy flavors. An excellent strong and full-bodied cigar.

Afternoon
Ramón Allones Petit Coronas. A classic mareva, it is fairly aggressive with earthy tones. A cigar that is definitely for a practiced palate with a preference for pronounced tastes.

Apéritif
Bolívar Belicosos Finos. An easier smoke than it used to be, this subtle, very flavorful campana (figurado) goes so well with champagne that it becomes sublime.

After a Light Dinner without Alcohol
Punch Double Coronas. A superbly made vitola; one of the greatest of its kind. It generates ample flavor and body, building towards mouth-watering spicy and honeyed modulations.

After a Light Dinner with Alcohol
Montecristo "A". A nice-sized gran corona (especial), with ample presence in the mouth. So intense and heady it can be overpowering.

After a Substantial Dinner with Alcohol
Partagás Pirámides Limited Edition. A superior Havana, all intensity and style. The rich range of spices demands and deserves much attention.

From top to bottom and left to right: Bolívar Belicosos Finos, H. Upmann Magnum 46, Partagás Série D N°4, Ramón Allones Petit Coronas, Punch Double Coronas, H. Upmann Sir Winston, Montecristo "A", Punch Super Selection N°2, Juan López Selección N°1, Partagás Pirámides Limited Edition.

GLOSSARY OF CIGAR TERMS

Binder: The tobacco leaf that binds the filler together, and is then rolled into the wrapper.
Blend: A combination of tobaccos of different strengths and flavors which makes up a particular cigar taste and smoking intensity.
Box: Whether natural or varnished cedar, this is generally the container in which cigars are packed and purchased. More specifically, the term box can be divided into boxes properly speaking and cabinet selections. Thus a cigar box, sometimes called a 13-topper or a flat-top, contains 25 cigars, with a row of thirteen atop a row of twelve. Cabinet selection cigars maintain their cylindrical form. Boxed cigars have a more squared silhouette.
Cabinet: Natural cedar or varnished, cabinets are square and contain a half wheel or quarter wheel of cigars. The cigars are almost always unbanded, but the entire half or quarter wheel is bound with a ribbon.
Cabinet Selection: A rectangular box that holds twenty-five or fifty vitolas. A typical packing technique in which cigars are bundled in three rows is known as 8-9-8.
Capa: Spanish name for the wrapper.
Cap: Small piece of wrapper leaf at the cigar's head.
Casa de tabaco: Highly aerated curing huts where tobacco is dried after harvesting.
Cepo: Spanish term for ring gauge.

Chaveta: A half-moon shaped metal blade used by *torcedores* to cut, shape, and flatten tobacco leaves.
Culebra: A model comprised of three small cigars braided together. *Culebra* means snake in Spanish. The psychoanalyst Jacques Lacan was a great fan.
Elephant's foot: A cigar with a small cylindrical head and a large flat foot. A specialty of Manila.
Envasador/Envasadora: Expert in arranging cigars for boxing.
Escogedor/Escogedora: The person who sorts cigars by wrapper color.
Escogida: Festival that takes place in Cuban plantation villages when *fábrica* experts select tobacco after the first fermentation.
Fábrica: The site of cigar fabrication and manufacture.
Filler: The cluster of tobacco at the center of the cigar (either rolled together "book" or "scroll" style, or pleated in the *entubar* method).
Finca: Farm or plantation where tobacco is grown.
Foot: The end of the cigar that you light.
Fumigation: Procedure consisting in eliminating all parasites present in tobacco.
Galera: Cigar rolling workshop. Often stamped on the bottom of cigar boxes. By extension, the technical name given to some cigar models.
Gavilla: The name for bundles of forty to fifty tobacco leaves before their first fermentation.

Guarantee seal: Official green paper seal affixed to boxes of Havana cigars assuring their authenticity and origin.
Half wheel: A bundle of fifty cigars held together with a ribbon. (*Media rueda* in Spanish.)
Hygrometry: The measure of atmospheric humidity. Hygrometers are often built into quality humidor's.
Head: The end of the cigar that you put in your mouth.
Humidor: A receptacle for conserving cigars, whether made of wood, glass, or other material. It can be as small as a jar or a box and as large as a room.
Matting: The buffing and dusting of wrappers with tobacco powder. A method that smoothes out a cigar's appearance, mainly practiced in North America.
Model: The format of a cigar, considered in terms of its shape, length, ring gauge and weight—not color.
Muñeca: Spanish for "doll," the small bunch of three or so tobacco leaves that the *torcedor* has just worked into shape for an individual binder and rolled into the binder.
Puro: Spanish name for a cigar. May also refer to a cigar made from one kind of tobacco leaf.
Quarter wheel: A bundle of twenty-five cigars, or a box containing them.
Ring: Also, cigar band or band. The small band of paper around a cigar. Originally intended for protection, it serves ornamentally and as a distinguishing mark for a brand.

Ring Gauge: (RG) designates the measurement of the diameter of a cigar. It is calibrated in sixty-fourths of an inch.
Roller: Common translation of *torcedor*.
Stripping: The removal of tobacco leaves' central veins.
Tapado: Large sheets of gauzy white cotton used to protect plants from overexposure to the sun. By extension, tobacco fields where these sheets are used.
Tercio: Name for the large bales of tobacco leaves after selection and second fermentation, before being shipped to *galeras*.
Torcedor: The person who rolls cigars.
Vega: Originally, tobacco field. Currently refers to specific plantation zones and vintage appellations.
Veguero: Tobacco plantation worker.
Vitola: From the perspective of the market, vitola refers to the brand/model/blend combination. From the perspective of production, it can be used synonymously with *galera*, and also refers to the hollowed wooden gauge used there to check cigar size. Thus, in its strongest sense, a cigar format or shape corresponds to a particular vitola production model. In a more general sense, each individual cigar can also be called a vitola.
Wrapper: The outermost layer of a cigar comprised ofahalf of a "de capa," upper-tier tobacco leaf. It must be as flawless as possible.

INDEX
The page numbers in italics refer to illustrations

Accessoires 53, 60–61
Ageing 50–51
Alcohol 64–65
Almuerzo 36
Altuglas 48
Arawaks 19
Arturo Fuente 12, 21
    Fuente Opus X Perfexción
    Robustos 86, *87*
Ashton 12
Auction sales 66–67
Bahia 19
Bahia Gold 18
Bances 15, 19
Baracoa 9
Bassinger, Kim 82
Bauza 12, 19
Belinda 14
Bertoua 21
Binder 92
Blend 92
Blumenthal, Dan 14
Bock, Gustave 44
Body 30
Body and Flavor 56–57
Bolívar 10, 26, 70
    Belicosos Finos 81, 90, *91*
Borneo 20
Boxes
    natural 40, 92
    traditional 40, 92
    varnished 40, 92
Brands 70–73
Brandy 64
Brazil 13, 19
Breña Alta 20
Brushing *50*
Cabañas y Carbajal 75
Cabinets 41, 92
Caldera del Tabariente 20
Calixto López 20, 66
Cameroon 13, 21
Campana 32
Canaria d'Oro 12
Canary Islands 20
CAO 18
Cap 92
Casa de tabaco 22, 92
Cases 60
Castro, Fidel 8
Centro fino 22
Centro gordo 22

Cepo 92
Cervantes 32
Champagne 64
Chaveta 24, 92
Chevaliers du Tastevin 67
Chlorophyll 30
Churchill 32, 72, 73
Churchill, Winston 82, *83*
Cifuentes 19
Cigar cutters 52, 61
Cigar punches 52, 61
Cigar rings 44–45,92
Cigarrito 36
Clarísimo 38
Claro 38
Clipping 52
Club des Parlementaires
    amateurs de havanes *63*
Cohiba 10, 26, 70
    Thirtieth Anniversary 75
    Coronas Especiales *35*
    Millennium 75
    Siglo I *37*
    Siglo III 88, *89*
Cojo 14
Colombus, Christopher 6, 9, 14, 19
Colorado 8
Colors 38–40
Connecticut 13, 19, 20
Consolidated Cigar
    Corporation 12, 20
Copaneco 14
Corojo 11
Corona (plant) 22, 38
Corona (model) 34
    grande 34
    gorda 34
Cortador 52
Costa Rica 14, 18
Counterfeits 68–69
Criollo 11, 14, 16, 18
Cruz Real 18
Cuaba 10, 70, *73*
    Exclusivos *35*, 55, *85*
    Millennium 75
Cuba 6, 8–9, 22
Cuba Aliados 15, 19
Culebra 92
Culture 22–23
Cut 52
Dalia 32

Danlí 14
Davidoff 12, 66
    80 Aniversario 75
Davidoff, Zino 12
Delicado 36
Demi-tasse 36
Diplomáticos 10, 26, 70
Dominican Republic
    12–13, 14, 19
Don Diego 12
Don Pepe 19
Don Ramos 15
Don Tomás 15
Double corona 32
Double Happiness 21
Drying 15, 22, *23*
Dunhill 12
    Cabinetta 75
    Havana Club 75
    Varadero 75
Dutournier, Alain 62

Ecuador 13, 14, 19
El Rey del Mundo 8, 10, 73
    Cabinet Selección
    Choix Suprême 84, *85*
    Taínos 86, *87*
Elephant's foot 92
Elizabeth I 6
England 6, 19, 46
Entreacto 36
Envasador 29
Escaparate 26
Escogedor 38, 92
Escogida 22, 24, 92
Estelí 16
Excalibur 15
Excelsior 18
Exquisito 32

Fábrica 24, 92
Fabrication 24
Fermentation 22, 24
Figurado 32
Filler tobacco 24
Finca 92
Flor de Copán 15
Florida 20
Foot 92
France 6
Fumigation 92
Galera (workshop) 26, *27*, 92

Galera (format) 26–27
Gastronomy 62
Gavilla 22, 92
General Cigars 12
Gérard Père et Fils
    222 78, 84, *85*
    444 78, 86, *87*
    555 78, 81, 84, *85*
    666 78
    888 78
    Cuvées spéciales 78–79
    Sélection des Sélections *51*
Gispert Petit Coronas
    de Luxe 75
Goldberg, Whoopi 82
Gran corona 32, 34
Guarantee seal 68, 93
Guillotine *28*, 52
H. Upmann 8, 10, 12, 26, 71
    Connoisseur N° 1 86, *87*
    Connoisseur N° 2 *37*
    Magnum 46 *35*, 81, 90, *91*
    N° 2 *33*
    Sir Winston 90, *91*
Habana 92/2000 11, 14, 16
Habana Gold 19
Habanos s.a. 69
Haiti 12
Harvest 22
Head 30, *31*, 93
Hecho a mano 25, 31
Hecho en Cuba 31
Hemingway, Ernest 65
Henry Clay 66, 75
    Diamantinos *74*
Hermoso n° 4 34
Honduras 12, 13, 14–15, 19
Hoyo de Monterrey 8, 10, 14, 71
    Épicure N° 2 81
    Le Hoyo des Dieux *35*, 88, *89*
Humidor 48
Hygrometry 46
Indian Tabaco Cigar 15
Indonesia 19, 20
Italy 6
Jalapa, valley 14, 16
Jamaica 19
Japan 6
Jars *47*
Java 20
Joaquín Cuesta 75
José Gener Magnum 40

José Luis Piedra 9
Joya de Nicaragua 16, 19
Juan Clemente 12
Juan López 10, 71
    Selección N° 1 90, *91*
Julieta 32
Kentucky 6, 20
Kingston 19
La Aurora 12, 21
La Corona *7*, 75
La Escepción *7*
    Longos 75
La Flor de Cano 67
    Diademas *75*
La Flor de la Isabela 21
La Flor Dominicana 12
La Gloria Cubana 10, 26, 70
    La Meridiana 16
    Médaille d'Or N° 1 84, *85*
    Médaille d'Or N° 2 *33*, 88, *89*
    Médaille d'Or N° 3 86, *87*
La Palma 20
Laguito n° 1 36
Laguito n° 3 36
Laura Chavin 12
Libre de pie 22, 38
Ligero 24, 30
Lighting up 53
Linnaeus, Carl 7
Listz, Franz 82
Llaneza, Franck 14
Lonsdale 32
Looks 54
Macanudo 12, 19
Machine 31
Madonna 83
Maduro 38
Magellan, Ferdinand 21
Malta 6
Manila 21
Mareva 36
Maria Guerrero *7*, 66, *75*
Maryland 6, 20
Mata Fina 19
Mata Norte 19
Mata Sul 19
Matting 93
Médici, Catherine de 6
Mexico 13, 18, 19
Minuto 36
Mitch, Hurricane 14, 16, 18
Models 93, 32–37
    large 32–33
    medium-sized 34–35
    small 36–37
    nonstandard 32
Moho azúl 11, 16
Moisture and Preservation 46–47
Mold 30
Montague 21
Montecristo 8, 10, 12, 26, 71
    "A" *33*, 90, *91*

Millennium 75
    Robustos 81
Montecruz 21
Moore, Demi 82
Morocco 6
Morocelí 14
Napoleon 7,82
Negro 39
Netherlands 6
Nicaragua 12, 16–17
Nicot, Jean 6
Nicotiana tabacum 7, 18
North America 53
North Carolina 6
Ocotal 16
Olor dominicano 13
Omotepe 16
Oriente 9
Oscuro 39
Padrón 16
    1964 Anniversary Coronas
    86, *87*
Padrón, José 16
Palacio, Fernando 14
Palmas reales 24
Panetela 36
Panetela larga 36
Partagás 8, 10, 12, 26, 72
    150th Anniversary 75
    155th Anniversary *33*
    Coronas Cabinet Selection
    88, *89*
    Cristal Tubos 75
    Lusitanias 88, *89*
    Palmas Reales Cristal Tubos 75
    Pirámides Limited Edition
    81, 90, *91*
    Salomones *33*
    Série D N° 4 81, 90, *91*
    Shorts 88, *89*
Partido 9
Peñamil 20
Petit corona 36
Philippines 21
Piloto cubano 13
Pinar del Río 11
Pirámide 32
Pleasure 55
Pléiades 12
Por Larrañaga 8, 10, 72
    Petit Coronas
    Cabinet Selection 86, *87*
Port 64
Price 66–67
Prominente 32
Punch 8, 10, 14, 72
    Double Coronas 90, *91*
    Super Selection N° 2 90, *91*
Puro 93
Quai d'Orsay 10, 72
    Imperiales 84, *85*
Quality, control 28–29

Quarter wheel 93
Rafael González 10, 73
    Coronas Extra 86, *87*
    Lonsdales *33*
    Petit Coronas 84, *85*
    Slenderellas 33
    Vitolas B 75
Raleigh, Sir Walter 6
Ramón Allones 8, 10, 12, 26, 73
    Coronas Cabinet Selection *35*
    Petit Coronas *37*, 90, *91*
    Small Club Coronas 81, 88, *89*
Reader 26
Remedios 9
Rum 64
Robusto 34
Roller 93
Romeo y Julieta 8, 10, 66, 73
    Belicosos *35*, 88, *89*
    Exhibición N° 2 *33*
    Romeos *75*
Russell Lillian 82
S.T. Dupont 20
    Robustos 81, 84, *85*
Saint Luis Rey 10, 73
    Churchills *33*
    Regios 88, *89*
San Cristóbal de La Habana 10, 73
    El Príncipe *37*, 86, *87*
    La Punta 88, *89*
San Juan y Martínez 11
San Luis 11
San vicente 13
Sancho Panza 8, 10, 73
    Belicosos 69
Santa Clara 18
Santa Damiana 12
Santa Rosa de Copán 14
Savoy, Guy 62
Savouring
    the art of 54
    body and flavour 55
    when the time is right 58–59
Seco 24, 30
Semi–Vuelta 9
Senderens, Alain 62
Scissors 52
Slide tops 41
Smell 54
Sosa 19
Sotheby's 66
Spain 7, 10, 16, 19
Stripping 92
Sucking machine 25
Suerdieck 19
Sula, valley 14
Sumatra 20
Sweet wines 64
Tabaco del sol 22
Tabaco tapado 22
Taino, tribes 6
Talanga 14

Tapado 22, *23*, 93
Taste 55
Types 57
Te–Amo 18
Temple Hall 19
Tercio 24, 93
Torcedor 24, 26, 27, 93
Totalmente
    a mano 25, 30
Touch 54
Très petit corona 36
Trinidad 10, *33*, 73
Tripa corta 31
Troisgros, Pierre 62
Turkey 6
Twain, Mark 82
United States 14, 19, 20
United States Tobacco 14
Uno y medio 22
V–shaped clipper 52
Vapor 26
Vargas 20
Vauquelin, Nicolas 7
Vega 93
Vega Fina 12
    Robustos 81
Vegas Robaina 10, 26, 73
Veguero 93
Vera Cruz 18
Villar y Villar 75
Vintage 74–75
Virginia 6, 20
Vista 42–43, 93
Vitola 93
Volado 24, 30
Vuelta Abajo 8, 10–11
Vuelta Arriba 9
West Indies 6
Whisky 64
Women and cigars 82, 83
Wrapper 24, 30, 92

Acknowledgments

To Anton Molnar and Antoni Vives Fierro,
for having introduced art into the world of the cigar
To my mother, for her example
To my wife, for her patience
To my sister, for her complicity
To Sévan and Taline, of course.

Photographic Credits
All photographs by Matthieu Prier, except the following:
pp. 4 and 6: all rights reserved; Gamma: p. 9, Ferri/Liaison; pp. 11, 23 right and 26, Marc Deville;
pp. 13 and 15, Franck Caradec; p.21, Mingasson/Liaison; 23 left, P. Siccoli;
p. 27, Jean-Marc Loubat.

Translated from the French by Chet Weiner and Stacy Doris
Copy edited by Christine Schultz-Touge
Box set presentation an original design by Open Door, UK
Originally published as *Le Cigare* © Flammarion S.A. 2001
English-language edition © Flammarion USA Inc. 2002
ISBN: 2-0801-0721-6
FA0721-02-II
Depôt légal: 4/2002
Printed and bound in Spain

Boutique Noga Hilton – 19, quai du Mont-Blanc – 1201 Geneva
Tel. + 41 22 908 35 35
Fax + 41 22 908 35 30
www.gerard-pere-et-fils.com
www.gerard.ch
info@gerard-pere-et-fils.com
info@gerard.ch